DEATH WAS MY NEXT STEP

A Child Raised by the Streets

Dixie Pebworth

ACKNOWLEDGMENT

First, I give all glory to God for the testimony He has written in my life. I pray that He might use this book to give hope to the hopeless and touch a dark and hurting world.

I would like to acknowledge my family and thank them for overlooking my mistakes and still loving me, supporting me, and inspiring me to fulfill my calling.

I would also like to acknowledge my spiritual fathers and their wives who helped me through the toughest times of my life:

Don and Dorma Bailey
Dave and Nancy King (Falling)
Ricky and Carla Musgrove
Maurice and Mary Kisler
Tony and Candy McMullen
John and Cassie Adams
Corky Pinkston
George Nowlin

To the Board of Directors and staff of Freedom Ranch, Inc.; the Board of Directors and staff of God's Shining Light Church; and the God's Shining Light Church family, I want to say, "I could never do it without you. May God richly bless you for your faithfulness."

DEDICATION

I dedicate this book to my dad, Joe Pebworth, who felt so strongly that my story would give hope to others, that he paid to have this book published before he passed away from cancer on June 6, 2011.

Death Was My Next Step
Dixie Pebworth with Bonnie Litterell
ISBN: 978-0-9889281-8-3
Copyright © 2013 by Dixie Pebworth

Published by Yorkshire Publishing
6271 E. 120th Court
Tulsa, OK 74134

Text Design: Lisa Simpson
www.SimpsonProductions.net

TABLE OF CONTENTS

CHAPTER 1

OCTOBER 7, 1987

WE, THE JURY, FIND THE DEFENDANT, DIXIE PEBWORTH ...

GUILTY! Count one: possession of a controlled, dangerous substance (Cocaine). We recommend a sentence of thirty years in the Department of Corrections.

NOT GUILTY! Count two: possession of sawed-off shotgun/ rifle.

GUILTY! Count three: possession of a firearm while in the commission of a felony. We recommend a sentence of forty years in the Department of Corrections.

GUILTY! Count four: possession of an illegal weapon (after former conviction of a felony). We recommend a sentence of ten years in the Department of Corrections.

I could hardly wrap my mind around what was happening. As I felt the life draining out of me, my knees buckled and I fell backwards into my chair. It was as if I were being swallowed up by the darkness by which I had lived. I don't remember what happened next in the courtroom or on the trip from the court-room to the "tank," as they called it in the Oklahoma County jail.

For five days, I lay lifeless on a flimsy, plastic-covered pad on a concrete floor that forty-five to fifty men shared with cockroaches and rodents. Voices in my head screamed at me, "Just kill yourself! It's over for you! You'll never be a husband to your wife, never a father to your children!" Tormenting thoughts of suicide swirled through my head and sickened me. I couldn't eat. I couldn't drink. I couldn't sleep. I was suffering intensely from the mental and physical agony of withdrawing from drugs as well as the realization that I had allowed my life to be destroyed from the inside out. I was so distraught that I hardly even noticed that five days had turned to nights and then back to daylight again. I was vaguely aware at times of the scratching and gnawing of the rats that nested underneath the shower floor—another terrifying reminder that my life had been destroyed. I began to agree with the voices in my head. Death would be better than this.

During my short bouts of sleep, I was plagued with replays of that nightmarish evening a few months earlier when the police kicked in the door to my house. On that night, March 5, 1987, I left my house around 9:30 p.m. to replenish my stock of drugs while some of my clients waited inside for me to return. On my way out of the neighborhood, I decided to stop at the corner store to pick up a six pack of beer and two packs of cigarettes. When I walked out of the store, I heard a car squealing around the corner. I looked up and saw it was a black and white police car followed by other black and whites, a van, a pickup, a Suburban, and two more black and whites—about ten cars in total. I watched the lead car turn and race down the block towards my house. Immediately, I rushed to the payphone and called home.

I had left a guy named George to answer my phone and door. When he answered, I said, "George, I don't want to scare you, but I need you to look outside and tell me where the ten police cars are that just came flying around the corner." George said, "Okay," and laid the phone down. The next second I heard the front door explode from the force of the battering ram the police used to gain entry. The next sounds I heard paralyzed me: my wife screaming; police yelling; M16 rifles cocking; and the hysterical cries of my two-year-old son. Guilt gripped me as I thought about my seven-day-old son that I had brought home from the hospital only three days before. He was so tiny and innocent and I had brought him into this madness. What had I done?

After the hysteria quieted, I was relieved that I hadn't heard any gunshots. I drove to a motel room to spend the night and waited about three hours before phoning my house again. When I called, my wife answered. She sobbed into the phone, "Dixie, the cops only want you! They said if you will turn yourself in, no one else will be arrested." She told me the police were angry that I wasn't there when they stormed the house. At first they accused her of being "Dixie," thinking that "Dixie" was a woman. I was relieved to hear that no one had been injured and that no one was arrested.

I turned myself in the next morning. The police bartered with me to give them five names and set up these five people to make a drug buy. They said if I cooperated with them, they'd let me go free. I wasn't a rat, never had been, and never would be. When I refused to give them any names, they processed me into the Oklahoma County jail and filed charges against me. My bond was high, somewhere around $50,000.

Not only had I made my family the victims of my drug habit, my wife at age nineteen, was suddenly facing a near empty cupboard with rent and utilities due the next week. I was the sole support of my wife, my two young sons, my mother-in-law, and my wife's aunt. Nightmares of what I had done to my family obsessed my sleep and tormented me as I lay lifeless on that filthy, tobacco-stained floor in the Oklahoma County jail. By the fifth day after my trial, I was in total agreement with those unrelenting, hellish voices in my head that shouted, "Go ahead! Kill yourself! Eighty years in prison! Your life is over! You'll never be a husband to your wife, never be a father to your children! You're already a dead man!"

Around 7:00 p.m. on the evening of the fifth day, an unusual thing happened. The lock on the cell door popped and a white-haired man stormed into the 30'x50' tank that had become home to me and forty-five other men. I sat up to see what was happening. Normally, the cell door was never opened after 5:00 p.m. The Baptist preacher who had entered the cell shouted, "I came here to tell you that God loves you." I looked around me. All the other inmates continued whatever they were doing as if the preacher hadn't said anything. As the preacher (who I'll refer to as Preacher Budd) began to tell about the love of God, my first thought was, "If God loves me, why am I here?" Preacher Budd never condemned me for being in jail. He only talked about the love of God. In his sermon, he read John 3:16: "For God so loved the world, that He gave his only begotten Son, that whosoever believeth in Him should not perish but have everlasting life." He continued with verse 17. "For God sent not His Son into the world to condemn the world but that through Him, the world might be saved."

The sermon continued in Luke 15. Preacher Budd read about the prodigal son and the parable of the sheep and how the shepherd would leave the ninety-nine sheep to go find the one that was lost. My heart was opened, and I felt I was receiving a message from God for the first time in my life. At the end of his message, Preacher Budd extended an altar call. With tears streaming down my face, I went forward to pray and give my life to Christ. All the darkness left me. I had peace! I had joy! I had forgiveness! I was amazed that these things I had sought, I found on my knees in the county jail. Preacher Budd explained that what had just happened to me was like a baby had entered my heart, but it was up to me to make him grow. The only way to make that baby grow was to feed him the Word of God.

I began reading God's Word eight to ten hours a day. Every time I opened the Scriptures, it wasn't about religion. It was about a relationship with God and knowing my Heavenly Father loved me, and that His love for me was greater than anything this world had to offer. Just as Preacher Budd had told me, the baby on the inside of my heart started growing. A light had finally come on inside of me and tears streamed down my face every time I read the Bible. The strange thing to me about my tears was that prior to accepting Christ as my Savior, I *never* cried. Drugs had hardened me, and I was downright mean. Prior to becoming a drug addict, I had always had a soft, caring heart. But drugs have a way of turning a soft, caring heart into a heart of stone.

My cellmates were watching me, and they saw a change in my life. Some of them thought I was crazy; others came over to talk to me out of curiosity; and some joined me for Bible studies. For the next two months, between my trial and the sentencing, all I did was read the Word of God. It's the only place I found peace in that overcrowded cell.

When I first started reading the Word of God, I'd have tormenting mental images reminding me of the things I had done in the past. One particular image, I remember all too well: At 3:00 a.m., I went to a guy's house who owed me a little over $500 for drugs. I kicked in his front door and went in with a pistol-grip shotgun. I caught him coming out of his bedroom in a long hallway. He hit the floor without a fight and screamed, "Don't shoot! Please don't shoot!" Somehow, the lights came on in the house. I looked up and saw the man's three sons sitting on the edge of their bed. Terror gripped them as I stood there holding a gun to their father's head. In the adjoining bedroom, the man's wife and four-year-old daughter were crying and screaming, "Please don't shoot! Please don't shoot! Please!" I backed away and left the house. Thank God, I didn't pull that trigger.

When these tormenting images of the kind of person I had become would come to my mind, I'd ask God to forgive me and I'd keep reading His Word. God's Word was like a shower cleansing me. Tears would stream down my face as I experienced His forgiveness and His overwhelming love.

My wife was allowed to visit me once a week, and she came faithfully on her visiting day. All we did was cry into the telephone receiver as we looked at each other through the plate glass. Over and over, I told her how sorry I was that I had ruined our lives and pled with her to forgive me. I wanted her to know that this had happened because of sin. At times I'd try to witness to my wife, but she wasn't interested in hearing about God or how I'd given my life to Christ. She had never been to church or even heard any teaching about God. Every day I prayed for her and my children. I prayed that God would provide for them and somehow get them out of the drug-infested neighborhood that I had made our home.

I turned twenty-four in jail a week after I committed my life to Christ. It was a hard day. There was no cake, no candles, no celebration. There was just the harsh reality of awaking in what I considered the lowest place on earth—a cement floor covered with filth and cigarette ashes in the county jail. I cringed as I shook the mouse droppings from my blanket, droppings left from the night before when the mice came out to search for any crumbs that might have fallen during commissary. *Happy Birthday to Dixie*, I thought.

A friend of mine knew it was my birthday, and he brought a new pair of tennis shoes to the jail for me. He had removed the innersole of one of the shoes, hollowed out a hole, filled it with marijuana, and then glued the sole back. The guards turned the shoes upside down and shook them. When nothing fell out or seemed out of place, they gave the shoes to me. I rolled the marijuana in small pin joints and sold them to get things I needed. But one night I decided to smoke one of them, and I got high.

After I smoked the joint, I had severe "cotton mouth," a term we used to describe the extreme dryness and discomfort in your mouth caused by smoking marijuana. Out of habit, I picked up my Bible and began to read, starting with the Gospel of John, Chapter 4. Jesus was talking to the Samaritan woman, and He said, "Give me a drink." The woman answered, "How is it that you, being a Jew, ask a drink from me, a Samaritan woman?" Jesus said, "If you knew the gift of God and who it is who says to you, 'Give me a drink,' you would have asked Him and He would have given you living water. Whoever drinks of this water shall never thirst again." As I read that scripture, the most amazing thing happened to me. My mouth suddenly filled up with so much water that I struggled to keep the water from gushing out. I sat straight up and looked around to make sure no one was playing a practical joke on me. No one was around or even paying any attention to me. I shook my head and looked back down at my Bible. I knew I had experienced a miracle right there in that county jail. I exclaimed, "God, You're real!" That was October 24, 1987—the last day I ever smoked marijuana.

Drugs had been such a stronghold for me. I had smoked my first marijuana joint, which was given to me by my teenage brothers, when I was only ten years old. I felt so grown up and cool to be included in the social life of the older boys, that I wanted a joint when my brothers smoked one. The boys gladly gave me the joints in exchange for my promise not to tell on them. To me, the marijuana joints were like the first grade of the drug world, creating in me a desire for stronger, more addicting drugs. Over time, drugs obsessed my life and became my dream of a successful career. But that day, October 24, 1987, in the Oklahoma County jail, God delivered me and I never touched drugs again.

After actually experiencing a miracle in my own life, I dove into the Word of God with a new fervor. As I continued to read about the miracles of Jesus in the New Testament, I began to feel that God would somehow intervene on my behalf. After all, I wasn't even there when the police kicked in the front door of the house. There was no evidence that proved the rented house, where the drugs and guns were found, was my home. My name was not on the lease, nor was my name on the utilities or phone. Even though the police found guns in the house, I wasn't there. I reasoned, "How could I possibly be in possession of a firearm if I wasn't there?" Not even my attorney thought I would be convicted.

I remembered reading a book while I was in juvenile detention the first time I was arrested at age fourteen. (This was the first book I had ever completely read from front to back.) The book , *Where Flies Don't Land,* was a true story of Jerry Graham, who was left with emotional scars from his painful childhood; he later committed murder and was given a life sentence. In prison, he found God and changed his life. God later delivered him from life in prison, and he was set free. I remembered thinking at that time, "If God is going to get my attention, He is going to have to do a miracle for me!" I didn't know at that time just how true that statement was.

I thought back to the morning of my trial. Jury selection began around 9:00 a.m. I don't remember most of the jurors except for a lady with a big, red Bible in her hand. Either the District Attorney or my attorney asked her, "What will you base your decision on?" She slapped her Bible and said, "I'll base it on the Holy Ghost!" My immediate reaction was to tell my attorney to replace her, but for some reason I changed my mind and didn't object to her being on the jury. Jury selection was completed by noon and the trial began at 1:00 p.m.

The trial only lasted two hours. My attorney didn't feel I needed to testify on my behalf because he didn't think the DA had enough evidence to convict me. The only evidence they had linking me to the house was a letter they found on the floor from my wife begging me to stop using drugs. My mother-in-law, who lived with us, testified that the guns in the house belonged to her. None of the other people testified who had been in my house that night when the police kicked in the door. The police testified of course, but their witness, the person I allegedly sold drugs to, didn't even testify. Around three o'clock, the jury went out to deliberate. Two short hours later, around 5:00 p.m., they came back with their verdict: a verdict of guilty on three of the four counts with a recommendation of eighty years in prison.

The judge asked my attorney if he would like to request a pre-sentencing investigation to decide whether the sentence should run consecutively or concurrently. My attorney asked the judge to grant the investigation, which pushed my sentencing date back approximately two months.

Looking back, I can see that the two-month reprieve was part of God's plan for me. During that time I read my Bible ten to twelve hours a day. I was always amazed at how chills would run up my spine and the hair on my neck would literally stand up as I read about Jesus casting out demons, healing the sick, and raising the dead. Tears streamed down my face when I'd read how Jesus fed 5,000 men and their families with only two fish and five loaves of bread—and there were twelve basketfuls of food left over! Every day I asked God to take care of my family, and every day He did.

God's love, evident in all the miracles, was so overwhelming to me that I read them over and over. I never saw the fear of hell. Every time I opened the Word of God, love seemed to ooze out of the pages. Jesus never talked down to sinners or condemned them. He never threatened them or tried to fill them with fear. Instead, He healed their sickness and delivered them from the oppressions of life. The only times that I found in the Bible that Jesus got upset with sinners was when He ran the money changers out of the temple, and when He called the Pharisees and Sadducees hypocrites and vipers for their lack of showing love and mercy.

Even in the darkest corner of the county jail, God's love flowed to me as I read His Word. At times, the atmosphere around me was so spiritually charged that I would weep in His presence. His love surrounded me and filled me. I felt that if I could just reach up a little higher, I could physically touch Him. I never knew a relationship with God could be like this.

I was especially touched with the story of the Samaritan woman at the well in John, Chapter Four. Jesus knew her faults and her shortcomings, but He did not condemn her. He offered her forgiveness and love. He did not shut her out of His life because of her past, but welcomed her with open arms. For the first time in my life, I really understood that God is a God of forgiveness—a God of miracle-working power—a personal

God—a God of love—and he loved me! His love was pure and clean, a type of love I'd never encountered before. His love was not based on what I did or didn't do—it was unconditional.

On December 1, 1987, the day before my sentencing, I lay on my bunk reading my Bible until around midnight before I drifted off to sleep. I knew God was real and already I had experienced his miracles in my own life—the miracle of His ongoing provision for my family and the miracle of filling my mouth with water when He delivered me from drugs. During the two months between my trial and my sentencing date, my encounter with God was so intense and so filled with love that I knew my Heavenly Father had it all under control. No matter what was going on behind the scenes, I felt God had a plan for me and that He would intervene on my behalf. I didn't know how he would intervene, but I felt He would do something.

CHAPTER 2

———

Iawoke early on December 2, 1987, and began reading God's Word around 5:00 a.m. I re-read the accounts of the miracles Jesus had performed when He was on earth: opening blind eyes, unstopping deaf ears, casting out demons, and healing the sick. I thought about the miracles God had performed for me the past two months in the county jail. Tears rolled down my face, and those chills that always amazed me began to run up my spine. God took me to Matthew 6:33, "But seek ye first the kingdom of God and His righteousness and all these things shall be added unto you." My faith soared. I thought about how I'd been seeking the Kingdom of God. The hair stood up on the back of my neck as it often did when God revealed his miracle-working power to me through His Word. I didn't know what He would do, or how He would do it, but I believed God would intervene for me.

The guards came to get me around 9:00 a.m. After hand-cuffing me and putting shackles on my ankles, they took me down in the elevator to the courtroom. As I stepped out of the elevator, I saw my wife holding our ten-month-old son. My mother, brother, sister-in-law, mother-in-law, and other family

members had also come for my sentencing. The guards immediately rushed me into the courtroom to stand before the judge,
and then my family was brought in.

After my family was seated, the judge asked the DA what
he recommended. The DA said, "We want the eighty years the
jury recommended." The judge then asked my attorney if he
had anything to say. My attorney replied, but I couldn't focus
on what he was saying. I knew I was guilty of sin, but I didn't
feel I deserved an eighty-year sentence. I was thinking, *I wasn't
even in the house when the police came, so how could they say I was
in possession of a firearm while committing a felony? Yes, I was a
drug addict and a drug dealer, but I haven't murdered anyone. I
don't deserve to have my life taken away!* All these thoughts and so
many emotions were running through my head. The judge then
looked at me and asked if I had anything to say. I wanted to say
something to the judge that would change his mind. I wanted
him to know that I had found a relationship with God and I
was a different person now. I opened my mouth to speak but
the Holy Spirit wouldn't allow me to say anything. My mind
went back to the day the jury announced their verdict and a
voice inside my head had spoken so boldly to me: "You knew
you were guilty!"

The judge began to sentence me. "Count one, possession
of a controlled, dangerous substance. I sentence you to thirty
years in the Department of Corrections. Count three, possession of a firearm while in the commission of a felony. I sentence
you to forty years in the Department of Corrections. Count

four, possession of an illegal weapon after former conviction of a felony. I sentence you to ten years in the Department of Corrections. These sentences will run consecutively for a total of eighty years in the Department of Corrections." The judge hit his gavel on the desk.

"Eighty years consecutively," resonated through my head. My mind cried out, *Where is God—the God I've been reading about? I thought He had a plan for me. I didn't know what, but I thought He would do something!*

Simultaneously, my family began sobbing. I felt as if my life was being ripped from my body—as if I was having an out-of-body experience. I could see myself standing there, but my spirit seemed to have left me. Tears streamed down my mother's face. Other times I had been arrested, she would rush to the jail and take me home. This time, she couldn't help me and it broke her heart. My wife trembled as she wept uncontrollably, clutching our young son. I felt as if I was at my own funeral—only I wasn't dead.

My body was so numb that my legs would hardly move when the guards spun me around to take me out of the courtroom. My wife looked up at me with terror-filled eyes as I stumbled past her. Everything inside of me cried out, *God, where are you?* I pleaded with the guards to let me comfort my wife, but they refused. I was glad my son was too young to know what was going on or why his father was in handcuffs and shackles.

The other inmates gathered around me when I was taken back into the cell. Many of them had been watching me turn my life around and were hoping for the best for me. A hush fell over the tank when I said, "I was sentenced to eighty years, consecutively." After a few minutes, inmates began coming to me and asking, "What are you going to do?" Each time, my answer was the same, "I don't know."

For the next thirty minutes, I sat like a zombie on my bunk where I had left my open Bible when the guards came to get me for sentencing. This time I didn't reach for my Bible. I felt like God had left me. The intense feeling of God's presence I had experienced for those two months between my trial and my sentencing was gone. Those hellish voices in my head began enticing me again to commit suicide, "Your life is over, you'll never be a husband to your wife, never be a father to your children. Eighty consecutive years—you're a walking dead man!" My sentence running consecutively meant that I'd have to serve the thirty years given for count one, then complete the sentence of forty years for count three, then finally start the ten-year sentence for count four.

After about thirty minutes, a guard came into the cell and told me I had a visit. My wife's twin sister was waiting to see me. My wife had already had her scheduled visit the day before, so she was not allowed another visit. The first thing my sister-in-law said to me was, "What are you going to do?" My answer was the same to her as it was to the inmates, "I don't know." Neither of us had much to say. What can you say to a person who has just been given an eighty-year sentence? Mostly, we just sat looking at each other through the plate glass. Near the end of the fifteen-minute visit, I told my sister-in-law to tell Ann, my wife, to read Matthew 6:33: "But seek ye first the kingdom of God and His righteousness and all these things will be added unto you." "It didn't do anything for me," I said, "but maybe it will do something for her."

I felt empty as I stood up to leave the visiting area. There was still no sign of God—no feeling of His presence or His overwhelming love that I'd found in those past two months in the county jail. On the way back to my cell, I ran into Preacher Budd. I told him what happened at the sentencing, and he looked at me with a bold stare and replied, "We're going to pray about this!" I'd learn later that the boldness he possessed was the holy boldness of a true believer. I didn't quite have that holy boldness just yet, but I sure did want it.

The guard returned me to my cell and I sat back down on my bunk. My untouched Bible still lay open on the bed. After about thirty minutes, Preacher Budd and another gentleman I didn't know, came to my cell to get me. We went into a small room and joined hands, and the gentleman began to pray. After he prayed, Preacher Budd prayed. By the time it was my turn to pray, tears were streaming down my face and I was clenching Preacher Budd's and the other gentleman's hands as I cried out to God from my Spirit. I felt as if I was experiencing birth pains—every fiber, every nerve ending, every part of my deepest being was groaning before the Lord. I needed answers. Jeremiah

33:3 was the first revelation I received from God when I started reading my Bible. "Call unto Me, and I will answer thee, and show thee great and mighty things, which thou knowest not." I needed to know that God hadn't abandoned me. I needed to hear His voice and feel His love again.

I asked God for three things as I poured out my heart to Him:

- The first thing I prayed for was to have a contact visit with my wife before I was taken to prison. "God," I prayed, "You said You are able to do exceedingly, abundantly above all I could ask or think, according to the power that worketh in us." (Ephesians 3:20) I couldn't get the frail, distraught image of my wife out of my mind as she stood weeping in that courtroom. I wanted to hold her and tell her that I loved her. I needed to ask her for forgiveness.

- The second thing I prayed for was that my wife and I would be reconciled and our marriage put back together—better than ever before. My sin and wrongdoing had destroyed our family, and I pleaded with God for another chance to be a husband to my wife and a father to my children.

- My third prayer request was for my freedom. I prayed God's Word back to Him, "God, you said if we ask, we will receive; if we seek, we will find; if we knock, the door will be opened to us." (Matthew 7:7-8)

I prayed for these three things in that exact order. As I got up to leave the room, nothing seemed to have changed inside of me. I didn't feel any different—I was still empty and void of the feeling of God's presence. However, I knew according to the Bible, God had taken us into His throne room when we prayed because His word says that where two or three are gathered together in His name, He will be in the midst of them. As I stepped through the door to go back into my cell, my sorrow lifted, and the most beautiful peace I've ever experienced filled my mind and filtered through my body. It was the "peace that surpasses all understanding" described in the Bible in Philippians 4:7. (NKJV) A smile came over my face because I knew God had heard my prayers. In time, I'd learn that God doesn't operate in the essence of minutes, hours, and days. He operates in God's perfect time. He may not always show up when we think He should, but He's always on time to accomplish His purpose in our lives.

I sat back down on my bunk, and again the guys gathered around me and asked, "What are you going to do?" I looked around to find my Bible, still lying on the end of my bed, and said, "I don't know what I'm going to do, but I know what I'm not going to do. I'm not going to stop reading this book!" As I reached over and picked up my Bible, I felt God's love sweep over me again.

December 2, 1987, my sentencing date, had been on a Wednesday. I awoke on Thursday morning hoping this would be the day that I'd have a contact visit with my wife—the day I would be able to comfort and hold her, but I didn't hear from her or anyone else in my family that day. Friday passed, then Saturday, then Sunday. County jail inmates sentenced to prison are rarely given the privilege of a contact visit. Their visitations are normally restricted to a telephone receiver behind plate glass with guards present. I kept reminding myself that God's Word said He was able to do exceedingly, abundantly above all we could think or ask. (Ephesians 3:20) As I continued to read God's Word, I felt He was saying to me, "Peace, be still." I was so thankful for His peace that surpasses all understanding.

On the fifth day after my sentencing, which was Monday, a guard came to my cell around 9:00 a.m. and said, "Pebworth, get dressed. The captain wants to talk to you." Prisoners were normally never allowed to go to a captain's office. I was afraid I was in trouble. Hopefully, none of my friends had tried to get drugs to me in the jail. When I walked into the captain's office, my wife was sitting there. The captain asked me if I knew this woman. I replied, "Yes, sir. This is my wife." The captain gave us fifteen minutes. Prayer request number one answered—my contact visit!

I immediately grabbed Ann and held her in my arms while tears streamed down both our faces. I told her how much I loved her and how sorry I was to have destroyed our family. I was shocked when Ann told me that the house we were living in had burned over the weekend, and our family had lost everything, but most importantly, no one was injured. "Thank God, thank God!" was all I could say. My three-year-old son had found the Zippo cigarette lighter engraved with my name that I had received for Father's Day earlier that year. He had taken the lighter into the back bedroom and set a basket of laundry on fire. He was so terrified that he ran out of the room and shut the door behind him.

The fire happened around 8:00 a.m. Saturday morning. By the time of our visit on Monday, my family was already in another house and God had replaced their furniture and clothing. God had protected my family and answered my prayers to get them out of the drug-infested neighborhood I had left them in. Ann proceeded to tell me that her mother had been praying for me and asked God, "Why are all these bad things happening to us?" In a dream, God showed her a vision of me praying and told her it was because I had prayed so hard. I was so grateful for the confirmation that God had heard my prayers.

The peace of the Holy Spirit filled me as I walked back to the tank. My entire face erupted into a beaming smile as I blurted out to my fellow inmates, "I had a contact visit with my wife! God answered my prayer!" I was filled with a joy only God can give someone who is facing an eighty-year prison sentence. The next day, guards came into the cell and told me to get my "bunk and junk." They were taking me to Lexington Assessment and Reception Center for evaluation to determine which prison in Oklahoma I would be sent to. I remember getting in the van and thinking to myself, "I'm on the road to my miracle." As we drove down Interstate 35, I looked outside and for the first time in my life, I saw the beauty of God's creation in the sky, the clouds, and the trees. I was seeing life like I'd never seen it before.

When I arrived in Lexington, I was put in a cell with an atheist; a tough guy who had been locked up for ten years but had recently escaped and had been recaptured. He swore there was no God and he was always mad because I wouldn't stop reading my Bible. There was nothing he could say or do to discourage me—the contact visit with my wife was proof to me of a living God and His power. I've never been one to back down when someone doesn't like what I'm doing, and I wasn't about to back away from reading God's Word. Day after day, he made fun of me. "Jesus freak," he taunted. One day, he told me that if I was going to survive in prison, I'd have to put down my Bible and prove I was a man. I replied, "I'll do whatever I have to do to survive, but I'll never stop reading my Bible." The atheist's face twisted into a snarl like a devil. I looked back down at my Bible and continued reading.

We were on "lock down" twenty-one hours a day in the assessment and reception center. During those twenty-one hours, we were only allowed out of our cell to do assessments, testing, physicals, and other evaluations. For approximately three weeks, I was locked up with this inmate I had come to think of as a raging demon. We were allowed to spend three hours a day in the day room, a large open area with a TV and table and chairs. I usually stayed in my cell and used the quiet time away from my cell mate to pray and seek God. Jeremiah 33:3 was my daily prayer, "Call unto Me, and I will answer thee, and show thee great and mighty things, which thou knowest not." God began to help me understand some of the things in my life that I had been questioning. I was reminded of an inner voice that had spoken to me when the jury announced my guilty verdict. A very clear voice inside me said, "You knew you were guilty." The jury didn't see Dixie Pebworth, a child raised by the streets. They saw inmate Dixie Pebworth, the criminal who'd been running wild since the age of fourteen.

I was born on October 19, 1963, in Oklahoma City, Oklahoma. My birth mother was only twenty-five years old when I was born and already had four other children, all with different fathers. I was definitely an unwanted addition to her family. To my knowledge, my birth mother never held me. My adopted mother came to the hospital and took me home with her when I was discharged. In my adopted family, I was the sixth child with three brothers ranging in age from five to fifteen and two sisters who were ten and twelve.

One of the earliest memories of my childhood was when I was about three years old. My adopted mother received a phone call that obviously upset her. She slammed down the phone and started yelling, "Grab Dixie. Get him to the back of the house quick!" She mumbled something about calling the police. From the back bedroom, I heard my brothers scrambling to slam the living room windows shut and heard the lock click on the front door. Above the chaos, I heard my mother's voice, "They are not going to take him! They are not taking Dixie." I began to cry. My three-year-old mind couldn't conceive that someone would try to take me. I heard the front door open and slam shut. I could hear my mother and another voice I didn't recognize yelling at each other on our front porch. After a few minutes, the voices quieted, and my mother came back into the house. Other than that episode, my life was normal during my first three years, but just after my fourth birthday, our life as a family drastically changed.

In December, 1967, my parents went out on a rainy night to celebrate my mom's birthday. Around midnight, my maternal grandparents came into our bedroom hollering, "Everyone get your stuff. You're going with us." Our parents' car had been rear-ended by a drunk driver. My dad was okay, but my mother was in critical condition with a broken neck. After two months, my mom was discharged from the hospital, heavily medicated and in a neck brace. For the next three to four months, she was bedridden at home. Even after my mother's neck healed, she never stopped taking prescription drugs—pain pills, nerve pills, sleeping pills, and mood enhancing pills. I remember distinctly how her affections and emotions changed as she became more and more dependent on the prescription drugs. I fought against the pills for her affection, but the pills won. Before the car accident, my mother would take us to the lake for the day, spend time with us, and attend school and sports functions, but as she took more and more drugs, she ceased being a mother to us.

She no longer did the normal mom things, such as breakfast, school lunch, cooking, laundry, caring for the family, etc.

My dad was a hard-working man, holding down two jobs to support our large family. On the weekends, my dad was busy with chores around the house and never spent much time with us. Saturday nights, my mom and dad would go out drinking and dancing. When my parents went out the front door, my brothers would go out the back door to hit the streets, me tagging along with them.

When I was eight years old, my sister's husband, who was in the Navy, was shipped out to sea for several months. My sister was in her seventh or eighth month of pregnancy, so she came home to have the baby. One night after the baby was born, I was awakened in the middle of the night and could hear my mother and sister in the living room taking care of my niece. I heard my mother say, "When I adopted Dixie…" I was stunned. I could hardly process what I had just heard. Finally, I decided to get dressed and confront my mother. I walked into the living room and asked if I was adopted. My mom looked at me and said, "No, you're not adopted." I said, "I just heard you say it." "Oh no," she said, "I was talking about the kid down the street." From that time on, a battle raged inside of me. Anger and insecurity fought to take over my mind. I knew what I heard. I couldn't trust my mother anymore because she lied to me. I felt betrayed and empty. So many questions swirled through my eight-year-old mind: *Where did I belong? Why didn't my real mother and father want me? Does anyone really want me?* On several occasions after that I'd ask my mother if I was adopted. She'd always lie and say, "No, I had you."

There were a few upsides to my home life. Our end of the summer routine was to go to a lake in Hot Springs, Arkansas. We'd spend two weeks in a cabin; fishing, swimming, and having fun. We got the chance to be regular kids. Aside from our regular vacations, the only time my father was involved in my life was to discipline me. It was always a strong hand of discipline done in anger, never a strong hand of love and correction.

By age nine, my nightly chore was to gather up my mother's dosage of about eighteen pills: Valiums, pain killers, Quaaludes, Placidyls, and other mood enhancing drugs. As my mother became more and more strung out on drugs, the streets became my parents.

On New Year's Eve, 1974, my parents went out to celebrate. I had just turned ten on my birthday in October of that year. My brothers and older cousins were in the back bedroom, and I was in the living room with a couple of younger cousins. I pushed my way into the bedroom and saw they were smoking marijuana and drinking beer. To keep me from telling on them, they offered me a joint and a beer. I got high, but went to sleep before my parents came home so they never found out. After that, I started stealing cigarettes from Mom's and Dad's packs. I wanted to be like my older brothers—cool and tough. By the age of eleven, I was smoking cigarettes in front of my mom. When she smoked, I'd grab a cigarette out of her pack for myself. All she said was, "You better hope your daddy doesn't find out!" Soon she started buying cigarettes for me.

In junior high school, I began skipping class. My mom knew I was skipping classes, but she didn't care. By now she had ceased being a mother in all respects; drugs were the only things that were important to her. She didn't care where we kids were. As soon as my dad was gone, we were on our own. If my dad found out that I had skipped school, he whipped me. Whipping me was all he knew to do. He punished me to try and make me better. But it didn't work—he had never spent any time with me, never showed me any affection, never taught me morals or how to be a man. All I knew to do was what I learned on the streets.

When I started high school, I wanted to play football. I had always had dreams of being a football player. I had a 3.85 grade point average the first semester of high school. But when football season was over, I began getting high on the way to school in the mornings with my brother Don and began skipping classes again. By now, Don had a girlfriend and didn't want me around anymore. One night Don beat me up and told me to go find my own friends.

I started hanging out with my friend's older brother John, who had previously lived in Chicago but had recently moved to Oklahoma City. He seemed so cool to me, and I looked up to him. He reminded me of the motorcycle riders I'd idolized at the age of four or five years old. My mom and dad would take me to the drive-in movies with them. They thought I was asleep, but I lay in the back seat with my eyes glued to the Hell's Angels movies they watched. Those movies, at my impressionable young age, built a desire in me to be a motorcycle outlaw or a gang member, roaming the streets and defying the police and other types of authority.

My dislike for the police started at the age of five. I was riding in a car with my mother when we saw a police car coming from the opposite direction. For no apparent reason, my mother started cursing the policeman. From then on, I thought the police, or anyone in authority, was my enemy.

The more hardened I became, the more intense my rebellion became. I was arrested for my first felony at the age of fourteen. Drugs controlled my life. I began to break into businesses and steal whatever I could sell easily to get more drugs. By this time, I was on a downward spiral and dropped out of high school.

One night, a month before my fifteenth birthday, my mother was high on drugs and started yelling at me to get her this and get her that. I was fed up with her and angry that drugs were more important to her than her family. I started yelling back at her, and we got in an argument. I knew the fair was in town and I felt I could get a job with the Carnies, so I walked out the door with only the clothes on my back. I stayed on the fairgrounds and left town with them when the fair was over. I enjoyed the gypsy lifestyle: traveling from town to town, meeting new people, and staying high on drugs. I continued my life of crime as we traveled around the country.

Eventually, at the age of eighteen, I was caught breaking into a Taco Bell for drug money and was sentenced to two years in prison. I served eight months and was then paroled. Drugs were unbelievably abundant in the prison, often smuggled in by the guards for money. I learned from other inmates how lucrative selling drugs could be. I went into prison as a burglar and a thief and came out a drug dealer.

As my drug business grew, my drug habit grew with it and so did my reputation with the police. Until that night the police kicked in my door, I had never stopped to think about the consequences of the lifestyle I was living. That night I realized for the first time that I had allowed drugs to destroy my life from the inside out.

Now, here I was at age twenty-four in an A&R center in Lexington, Oklahoma, being evaluated to see in which prison I would spend the rest of my life. I believed God would allow me to go to Joseph Harp, a nearby medium-security prison where I could be close to family. I definitely didn't want to go to Dick Conner Correctional Center in Hominy, Oklahoma. It was considered a gladiator school for criminals, with fights daily, beat downs weekly, and at least one stabbing or killing per month.

My security points from my assessments at Lexington A&R allowed me to go to a medium-security facility, which would be either Joseph Harp or Conner. When they classified me, I was told that I would be going to Joseph Harp. The next day I was told to get my "bunk and junk" to be processed out. As I got in the van, I asked the guard where we were headed and he answered, "Conner prison." I said, "Oh no! I can't go to Conner. I'm classified to go to Joseph Harp!" I immediately stood up and started to get off the van. The guard shoved me back down and said, "You're going to Conner, boy!" He slammed the door in my face.

CHAPTER 3

—◦◦◦—

All I remember about the three hour drive to Conner prison in Hominy, Oklahoma, was the squeezing pain in my chest and the fear that wrestled to suck my breath away. I sat staring out the window but seeing nothing. My mind screamed, *God, not Conner, not the gladiator school. God, I don't want to go to Conner!* The atheist inmate's statement resonated through me with every pump of my heart, "One day you'll have to put down that Bible and prove you're a man." I had told him, "I'll do what I have to do to survive, but I'll never put down this Bible." Satan taunted, "He's right—you'll find out! Your Bible won't do you any good at Conner. You'll never get out alive!"

We pulled up to Conner around ten o'clock at night. The building was lit up like a Christmas tree—big lights, gun tower sitting on the edge of the fence, and razor wire all the way around. Conner prison housed over one thousand male inmates; half of them would never make it out alive. Many of them had committed the most heinous crimes you can imagine to get there. As I stared at what I perceived to be a small replica of hell, I thought, *Somehow, I've got to go in there and survive!*

As we entered the prison, there were about fifteen guys standing around. Some were there to help us get our mattresses and guide us to our cells. Others appeared to be sizing us up. The guard told me to go to C120 and handed me a mattress. Conner prison was divided into several units with 160 inmates in each unit. I followed my escort across the prison yard with my mattress over my shoulder. Cradled in my right arm, I carried a small box with my Gideon paperback Bible and a few personal things. As the lock to my cell popped open, I could see the inmate inside my cell was high on drugs. "God," I prayed, "I don't want to be in this cell with him. I don't want drugs in my life anymore. All I want is Jesus and to change my life and hurry up and get out of here." I knew that if God heard my prayer once, He would hear it again.

I climbed onto the top bunk and took out my Bible. My cell mate kept interrupting me to tell me about the prison, the other inmates, the guards, and the rules. I told him I didn't care to hear about the prison; I only wanted to read my Bible. He finally went to sleep. The next morning around 6:30 or 7:00, the guards removed him from the cell. He had gotten in trouble the night before and was taken to "lock up." I was grateful to have the cell to myself for a few days to give me time to read my Bible and hear from God.

The next morning, which was a Saturday, I went to breakfast at the chow hall. Even though it was December, I was sweating as I walked across the prison yard. In prison, you have to be aware of your surroundings and who is around you at all times.

Some inmates stared at me in curiosity; others tried to intimidate me with their glares and obvious hardness. I tried to appear calm and fearless, but inside my mind was churning, *Somehow, I've got to make it out of here alive! Somehow, I've got to survive!*

I hurried back to my cell to read my Bible, then went back to sleep till lunch time. After another uncomfortable meal at the chow hall, I decided to look for a schedule of chapel services. There wasn't a chapel at Conner prison at that time, just a room in a building where church services were held. As I walked past the window of the chapel area, I realized they were having a chapel service. I went in and sat down on the front row. A Baptist church was hosting the service, but they allowed the inmates to be in charge. Inmates were giving their testimonies, preaching mini sermons, and singing songs. One of the inmates, George, sang like an angel. He was singing, "Touch Your People Once Again." The song spoke of the mighty rushing wind of God blowing to heal His broken and wounded people. I began to weep as that mighty rushing wind of God's Spirit touched me once again.

Then another inmate, Corky, preached a thirty minute sermon in ten minutes. I wept the entire time Corky was preaching. God was reaching out to me, and I desperately needed to hear from Him. Another inmate gave his testimony of how God had worked in his life during the five years he had been at Conner. I began to weep again, thinking, *I can't live here for five years. I can't take it!* The inmates gathered around me, prayed, and shared scriptures with me.

I walked back to my cell, still struggling with fear. All I could think was, *God, I want to go home!* I got down on my knees in my cell and prayed in desperation, "God, why didn't you stop me? Why didn't you show me you were real before I destroyed my life?" God simply said, "I tried. You wouldn't listen." I jumped up off my knees. "God, when did you warn me? When did you try to show me you were real?" I questioned.

I was led by the Holy Spirit to read two Bible verses. The first scripture was 1 Peter 5:8, "Be sober, be vigilant; because your adversary the devil, as a roaring lion, walketh about, seeking whom he may devour." God showed me I had an enemy—an enemy that was very real, although I couldn't see him. The second scripture was John 10:10, "The thief cometh not, but for to steal, and to kill, and to destroy." *Okay*, I thought, *but if I can't see him, how will I know when he's there?*

As I thumbed through the pages in my Bible, John 14:26 caught my attention. Jesus was speaking. "But the Helper, the Holy Spirit, whom the Father will send in My name, He will teach you all things, and bring to your remembrance all things that I said to you." Memories began to fill my mind.

My grandmother, who lived two hours' drive from us, was the only godly influence I'd experienced as a child. We went to see Grandma maybe three to four times a year: usually Christmas, the summer family reunion, and maybe a couple other holidays. I remember how happy Grandma was – always singing gospel songs while she cooked and did the dishes. Sometimes

Grandma would talk to me about Jesus and Grandpa would roll his eyes. *That was Satan*, I thought, *stealing away the stories Grandma told me.* When Grandpa rolled his eyes, it made the stories seem like a fairy tale.

When I was about ten years old, I answered a knock at the door. A young man stood there holding a new, leather-bound football. He told me I would get a football if I would get up Sunday morning and ride the bus to church. I had hopes and dreams of playing football someday, so I was on that bus. I was so disappointed and angry when the church gave me a cheap inflatable football instead of the nice, leather-bound ball that was brought to my door. I felt I'd been deceived and vowed I'd never go to that church again. Every time I saw their church bus in my neighborhood, I would hide, and if they came to the door, I wouldn't answer. *Ah, there he was again,* I gasped. This time Satan was using disappointment to keep me from knowing God.

One day when I was in high school, I was watching a class-mate weld. As I looked through the welding hood, I started thinking of hell's fire that my Pentecostal grandmother had often talked to me about. I was high on drugs and felt like I was falling into the flames. I ran out of the welding booth shaking my head. That horrible image of hell was a frightening experience and really made me think about my life. But after a couple of days, I reasoned, *That's just "religion" talking – that "hell" stuff!* I shook it off and started getting high again. Satan has lied to so many people, making them believe that anything to do with God and hell is just "religious" talk. By the time they find out the truth, Satan has brought so much hurt into their lives. Sadly, some don't find out until they die and enter the gates of hell!

When I was fifteen, a parole officer felt sorry for me and sent me to a group home that was amply staffed with trained counselors and housed about fourteen troubled boys. The counselor that worked one on one with me took me to church with him. I got along great with my counselor and started to deal with the issues in my life. But then I got angry about something and blew up and wasn't allowed to stay at the group home after that.

After leaving the juvenile group home, I was sent home with my parents while I waited for a court hearing. It was then that Satan launched an emotional blow that sent me back out into the world of crime that didn't end until I met Jesus in the county jail. The judge was doing a presentencing investigation and my mom called me from work and told me to get my birth certificate out of the red box in my parents' bedroom where valuable papers were kept. I found my birth certificate, but I also found my adoption papers. I was holding the proof in my hands. I was adopted, and I had been lied to over and over by my mother. The truth was: I was abandoned, rejected by my birth parents – a bastard child! I couldn't even trust my own mother to tell me the truth and help me understand. All I knew at that moment was, *I've got to get out of this house. I can't stay here.* I vowed when my court hearing was over, I would leave again and this time I wouldn't be back.

I received probation from the court, but I didn't stay around to meet with my probation officer. I didn't tell my mom I had found the adoption papers, but when my parents weren't home, I laid the adoption papers on top of the red box so they would know I knew the truth. This time anger – another one of the weapons in Satan's arsenal – erased all the desire to turn my life around that had been instilled in me by the juvenile center counselor. At age fifteen, I only knew one place to go, and that was to rejoin the carnival. I soon returned to my life of drugs and crime.

As I looked back at my life, I could see that every time I would get close to really knowing God and changing my life, Satan would bring in his arsenal of weapons – lies, anger, bitterness, disappointment, unforgiveness, the lure of alcohol and drugs (a major tool of his), peer pressure (looking cool and tough) – to name a few. I'd let my emotions take over, and I'd go spiraling back to my old lifestyle of drugs and crime.

But, still, God did not give up on me. The strongest warning came two months prior to the police kicking in my door in March 1987. My parents had gone to my Pentecostal grandmother's house for Christmas. When they returned, my mother called me and said, "I don't know what you are doing, but Grandma is worried about you." I said, "What do you mean Grandma is worried about me? Grandma doesn't know anything about what I do!" My mother quickly said, "Well, I don't know what is going on, but I know Grandma is worried about you and she's praying for you!" I said, "Okay," but I thought to myself, *Grandma don't know anything.* Boy, was I wrong; Grandma did know something!

The Lord showed me, through my grandmother, that He was not only warning me about the direction of my life but that it was my grandmother's prayers that saved my life the night the police kicked in my door. It was not a coincidence I walked out of the house two minutes before the police arrived. Had I been in the house, I would have been in the back room preparing the drugs for my customers. I had a gun in my top dresser drawer and one under my mattress. I would have thought we were being robbed, and in the commotion, I would have run out of the backroom with my gun and the police would have shot me.

My wife had also written me a letter begging me to stop taking drugs. Even though I was too strung out on drugs to see that I was destroying my life from the inside out, my wife recognized it and begged me to stop. The police found her letter lying on the floor when they kicked in our door and used it for evidence in my trial.

After my arrest, it took my wife two weeks to raise enough money to get me out on bail. But even then, I returned to selling drugs because by now it was the only thing I knew to do to support my family and my $500 a day cocaine habit. One night I had used the last of my cocaine; at 3:00 a.m., I was "feening hard" (a slang term meaning desperate for drugs). I looked at my wife who was sleeping beside me and thought about my two sons in the adjoining bedroom. For the first time I realized, *I've destroyed my life. Drugs have destroyed me from the inside out.* I thought about my grandmother and her prayers for me. Then I remembered a little Gideon Pocket Bible I had seen in my top dresser drawer. I didn't know how it got there, but I opened the drawer and began to read it. I remembered saying a prayer and asking God to restore everything I had destroyed. After praying, I went to sleep, but the next morning I continued using and dealing in drugs—right up to the time of my trial in October 1987.

God showed me that He has a plan for each of our lives, but Satan also has a plan for our lives. God has a plan for us for good; Satan's plan is to steal, kill, and destroy us and those we love. Just like God brings people and events into our lives to lead us to Him, Satan brings people and events into our lives to lead us into destruction. I don't believe it was God's divine plan or choice for me to go to prison; I went to prison because of the choices I made, but God never gave up on me. He was always reaching out to me and preparing my heart for the day I would finally listen—the day Preacher Budd would storm into that jail cell and proclaim, "I came here to tell you God loves you!" I had spent my life until then following Satan's plan. I was ready to consecrate my life to God and discover His divine plan.

Finally, I exclaimed, "Okay God, you tried to warn me!" I dropped to my knees. I knew I had to separate myself from the things of the world. Romans 12:2 says: "Be not conformed to this world but be transformed by the renewing of your mind." I reasoned, *If you are transformed by the renewing of your mind, then you are conformed to this world by the use of your mind.* I realized the impact the world has on your eyes and your ears; it affects your heart and thought life. I set out to guard myself from the demonic warfare that had destroyed my life by refraining from watching TV or listening to secular music. As a fast before the Lord, I decided that the only liquid I would drink was water my first year in prison. I vowed to "Seek ye first the Kingdom of God and His righteousness and all these things shall be added unto you." (Matthew 6:33) I needed a miracle. Somehow, I had to survive. I had to make it out of this gladiator school alive!

Once again, I felt God's peace that surpasses all understanding as I got up off my knees. I'm glad I didn't know at that time that Satan would set in motion a chain of events that would cause a "kingpin" of one of the prison drug rings to rise up against me.

CHAPTER 4

"Pebworth, report to the visitation room." I jumped to my feet. *Have I only been here two weeks?* I thought, as I held myself back to keep from running down the hall. *It feels more like two months!* I couldn't wait to hold my wife in my arms, tell her I love her, and apologize again for destroying our lives. The first person I saw as I entered the visitation room was my mom. She hugged me and told me she had come to the county jail to see me after my trial, but I had already been transported to Lexington A&R. My dad also hugged me, looked into my eyes, and said, "Son, I think you've been done wrong." Then for the first time in my life, he told me he loved me—bittersweet words to hear for the first time at age twenty-four in prison. After greeting the family friend who had come with my parents, I looked around for my wife, but she was not in the visiting room. My mom explained that she had come with them, but had not been allowed to enter the prison because she didn't have the proper identification.

I went out to the yard and saw Ann standing near the fence. I ran over to her and yelled, "I love you!" through the razor wire. She was crying as she yelled back, "I can't do this. I can't wait for you." Her family and friends were telling her that she needed to go on with her life. She felt there was no hope that I'd ever get out of prison. A guard rushed over and ordered my wife away from the fence, telling her she had to wait in the car.

As I watched my wife walk away, every hope I had managed to hold onto was stripped from me. I thought, *There's no reason to live. Without her and my sons, why fight to make it out of this hell hole?* I struggled to hold back my tears and despair for the next four hours of my family's visit. As I walked back to my cell, the darkness of deep depression settled over me. There were those voices in my head again: "You'll never get out—never get out—never make it out alive!" My wife continued to write to me, but her letters were heartbreaking. She would say the kids were fine and that her family was fine, but never anything personal except that she was going on with her life and that she had enrolled in college. I'd write back and she would answer with a one page letter, never giving me any reason for hope.

I tried to talk to the prison counselors to see if there was any hope for me. They told me the very earliest I could possibly come up for parole was February 1997—and that would only be on my thirty-year sentence. If I was paroled, then I'd start my forty-year sentence. Since this was only January 1988, the counselors refused to continue any discussion of parole with me. My attorney had filed an appeal on my behalf, but I was told that the appellate system was so backed up that it would take years to get a hearing.

The first six months I was in prison, all my friends turned their backs on me. My mom and dad came to see me about every three to four months. My wife only came to see me once in 1988. The only encouragement I received from anyone was a card with $10 in it every month, signed, "Don't give up. Mom."

After a while, I gave in to the hopelessness and slipped deeper into the hellish grip of dark depression. God began to deal with me to rise above my despair. I said, "God, what about my family?" He gave me two scriptures. The first was Genesis 12:1–3: "Now the Lord had said unto Abram, Get thee out of thy country, and from thy kindred, and from thy father's house, unto a land that I will shew thee: And I will make of thee a great nation, and I will bless thee, and make thy name great; and thou shalt be a blessing: And I will bless them that bless thee, and curse him that curseth thee: and in thee shall all families of the earth be blessed."

The second scripture was Galatians 2:20: "I am crucified with Christ, nevertheless I live; yet not I, but Christ liveth in me. And the life which I now live in the flesh, I live by the faith of the Son of God, who loved me and gave Himself for me." God told me that if I would seek His face and the knowledge of His grace, He would bring my family back to me when it was time.

To fight the depression, I started reading a chapter in my Bible every morning; when I woke up, I'd roll over and read God's Word to help me get out of bed and face another day. I continued to consecrate myself to God by refusing to watch TV or listen to secular music. I also continued my fast of drinking only water for that first year in prison. I read my Bible and sought God—I was fighting for my sanity and my life. I knew God was my only answer.

The Christian friends I had made at my first chapel service continued to be an encouragement to me. Corky and George would throw scriptures at me and they always seemed to quote exactly the ones I needed to hear. Rhema Bible Training Center in Broken Arrow, Oklahoma, offered free correspondence courses for prisoners, so I enrolled in their three-year program. As I obeyed God and sought His face, He began a supernatural transformation inside of me. Satan had tried to destroy my life from the inside out. God was giving my life back to me—from the inside out.

Although Conner prison was known as a gladiator school, it had one of the best chapel programs in the state of Oklahoma. There were chapel services three times on Saturday, three times on Sunday, and every night of the week. I attended all of them. Each time the altar was opened for prayer, I went forward to have someone pray with me.

After a while, I began to get confused. There were the Baptists, Pentecostals, Catholics, Methodists, Charismatics, Episcopals, Nazarenes, Church of Christ, and a few others. One group would say healing was for today and another group would say healing had been done away with. In another service, the sermon would be that the gifts of the Spirit are for today and then the next service the sermon would be that the gifts of the Spirit ceased when Jesus and the Apostles died. In one service, the ministers would pray that God would set the captives free; another minister would tell me it was wrong for me to pray to get out of prison because it was God's will or I wouldn't be there. The sermons were contradicting and it confused me.

One night I went back to my cell so confused that I got down on my knees and asked God for direction. The Lord led me to John 14:6, "I am the way, the truth, and the life; no man cometh unto the Father, but by Me." God showed me that in all these denominations there is a slice of truth and people who walk in the sincerity of their heart, but they only walk in the light they are taught. When you put them all together, you have truth. When the denominations begin to divide His body and stop walking in love, they miss God.

God told me to be kind and gentle to people in other denominations and to attend the services I wanted to attend, but to sit on the back row. As long as they followed the Word of God, I could follow them. If they stopped following the Word of God, then I was to stop following them, based on John 14:6.

Jesus is the only sacrifice that was ever given for our sins. Although a person can have differing beliefs about doctrine, they must receive Jesus as their sacrifice for sins in order to go to heaven. Many beliefs of the world today are the result of man trying to reach God. Judaism, Buddhism, and Hinduism are all reflective of man trying to reach God. But only in Christ is God reaching out to man. The Bible says that every knee shall bow and every tongue shall confess that Jesus Christ is Lord.

Through this revelation from God, I was able to put my mind at rest and enjoy attending various chapel services. In addition to the three-year correspondence course I was taking through Rhema Bible College, I also enrolled in some theology classes at Oklahoma Baptist University.

I wasn't expecting a visit on Father's Day 1988, but when I received notice to report to the visiting room, I was surprised to see my wife, Ann, and my two sons, Little Dixie and Cory, waiting for me. The moment Little Dixie, my three-year-old, saw me, he ran and jumped in my arms and started hugging me. I hadn't seen him since my trial in October 1987. My wife didn't bring him to the courthouse for my sentencing because we didn't want him to remember seeing his dad in handcuffs and shackles. It was bad enough that he would have to spend the rest of his life visiting his dad in a room full of strangers.

As I walked over to Ann, she said, "Here," and shoved Cory, my sixteen-month-old son, in my arms. She said, "I only came so you could see your sons." She walked over to the corner and sat down refusing to talk to me. Cory had a fever and blisters covered his lips. I held him and prayed for him for about two hours, speaking the blood of Jesus over him and asking God to heal him of the fever.

After two hours, I felt the fever leave him. He wanted his bottle, but it was empty. I walked over to Ann and asked her to fill his bottle with water from the fountain. She snapped, "He won't drink it!" I said, "Please, just fill up the bottle." My son drank the whole bottle in a matter of minutes. I walked over to her holding up the empty bottle and said, "I thought you said he wouldn't drink it." She was surprised and said, "What did you do to him?" I answered, "Nothing. I just prayed for him." She shook her head. At that time she didn't know anything about God. I don't know if she even believed there was a God. She had never had any teaching or any exposure to spiritual things. I asked her to refill the bottle and Cory drank another full bottle of water.

I spent the entire visit enjoying my sons—playing, wrestling, and laughing with them. Ann stayed in the corner and didn't say much, but she noticed there was something different about me. I wasn't angry and cussing or trying to control her. She gave me a little side hug when they left, but gave me no indication that I'd ever see her again. Little Dixie and Cory kept looking back at me and crying. As I watched the door close behind them, an onslaught of emotions overwhelmed me—feelings of emptiness, guilt, shame, regret, separation, rejection, hopelessness, and abandonment. I felt like heavy buckets of lead had been attached to poles that I was carrying across my shoulders causing me to only be able to walk in slow motion back to my cell. I tried to conceal my feelings as I walked past the other men. I had learned it's unwise to show weakness in a prison. Thank God my cell mate was not in the cell when I arrived.

I fell on my knees and cried out to God. The pain was too great; I couldn't bear it alone. I had to get back in God's presence, "the secret place of the most High and abide under the shadow of the Almighty," as stated in Psalms 91:1.

During my first year in prison, I had built a personal relationship with God through faithfully reading my Bible, praying, and attending the chapel services at the prison. It was in that "secret place" in God's presence that I learned to release my past, my future, my hurts, and my emotions. It was the place where I learned that even though I was surrounded with negativity and the presence of evil, I could walk in peace across the prison yard with my Bible in my hand and sing from a joyful heart. Psalm 16:11 says, "Thou wilt shew me the path of life: in thy presence is fullness of joy; at thy right hand there are pleasures for evermore."

I also learned to hear and recognize the voice of God in that "secret place." John 10:27 says, "My sheep hear my voice, and I know them, and they follow me." Like the Prophet Elijah, in 1 Kings 19:11–12, I learned that God often speaks in a still, small voice. I still seek that voice today in the decisions I make and the things I do. It's the same voice that I learned to hear in the county jail and in prison—God's still, small voice that consoled, strengthened, and led me. It's the same powerful voice that spoke light into existence. When God speaks to me, it expels the darkness, and "I know that I know" that I've heard from Him.

I learned so many things during that first year in prison. It was a time of inner healing and preparation for the ministry God has for me today. During that time, God helped me accept the fact that I was adopted and that although I had never known my real mother and father, I was a child of God. God was my Father and that heritage was greater than any earthly father could ever give me.

I continued to write to my wife for several months after the Father's Day visit. A minister who came to the prison to hold chapel services counseled with me and gave me some guidelines to follow in my letters. He advised me to always encourage and uplift her; not to make accusations or try to control her; to speak of mercy and forgiveness; and to let the love written about in I Corinthians, Chapter 13, be the guidelines for my letter. I told her I loved her, asked her to forgive me, and told her I was there for her if she ever needed me. I kept my letters positive, telling her I was taking GED classes and updating her on my progress of the correspondence courses I was taking through Rhema Bible Training Center.

In August 1988, I received a letter stating that Plattsmouth, Nebraska, had a warrant on me and that I was to be transported to Nebraska after my release in Oklahoma. I had gone to Nebraska previously to get some marijuana plants, which grew wild there. The marijuana plant was used to make rope, but it was illegal to cultivate or gather plants and transport them. I was arrested in Nebraska with my pickup bed full of marijuana. I signed a document to allow Nebraska to accelerate their time to transport me there for a hearing.

Plattsmouth had a very small county jail. There were no church services, but I continued to read the Word of God, spend time in prayer, and began to read spiritual books. The thought occurred to me that I could escape easily from there, but the Spirit of God wouldn't let me try. The leader of the AA group in Plattsmouth was also a Boy Scout platoon leader. During an AA meeting, I shared my testimony, and he asked me if I would talk to his Boy Scout group. The county sheriff allowed him to bring the boys to the jail, and I shared my testimony with them. I told them I had been sentenced to eighty years in prison and told them they never wanted to do drugs or wind up in prison. That was the first time I saw that God could turn everything around for good and use my life to touch others.

I went to trial in Nebraska and was sentenced to fifteen months, which was to run concurrently with my Oklahoma time. My flight back to Hominy, Oklahoma—handcuffed, in a single engine plane—was an experience I hope to never relive. I was actually relieved to arrive back at Conner prison! At the end of fifteen months, I was amazed to receive a check in the mail for $100 from the State of Nebraska due to a law that says when a person is discharged from prison and they have no money on their books, the state must give them $100. The money enabled me to get some things I needed—another of God's miracles in my life.

On New Year's Day, 1989, I was told to report to the visitation room. I had no idea who might be visiting me. I had stopped writing my wife several months previously because there was no response from her. I released her to God and asked Him to bless her and help her put her life back together. I had received a Christmas card from her but no other correspondence.

When I walked into the room, Ann was sitting there. I looked around and said, "Where are my sons?" She replied, "I came to visit you." "Oh really," I said, "What brought this about?" She explained, "I'll tell you the truth. I went to a New Year's Eve dance last night. At midnight when the guys kiss the girls, I looked around for the guy who took me to the dance. He wasn't there. I went outside and looked up at the sky and said, 'God, where is my man?' He said, "He is at Hominy, Oklahoma, in Conner prison." She continued, "I never forgot how much you had changed when I came to visit you on Father's Day. There was something different about you—something wasn't the same. So I wanted to come see for myself." Ann had not become a Christian yet, but through AA she had learned that there was a higher power and she believed it was God. For the next eight hours, we cried, laughed, talked, and enjoyed each other.

For the next three years, my wife never missed a weekend coming to see me—usually both Saturdays and Sundays. She had been able to buy a little Toyota car with her income tax refund and had started working for a marble company. Her boss had given her a gas credit card as part of the benefits on her job and told her she could buy as much gas as she needed. Her boss didn't know she had a husband 120 miles away in prison—but God did. I remembered God's promise to me, that if I would read His Word and seek His face, He would bring my family back to me when it was time. The gas card made it possible for Ann to visit me whether or not she had a dime in her pocket. Some days we couldn't even afford a Coke from the machine, but God had made a way for her to always have gas for her car.

In April 1989, Ann was going through some hard times. I went to a chapel service on a Tuesday night and requested prayer for her. Pastor Ricky prayed for Ann and asked me if I would like for someone in his church to visit her. I said, "Would you?" He replied, "As a prison volunteer, I'm not supposed to, but I will." I gave him Ann's address and phone number. Pastor Ricky and his wife went to visit her and led her to the Lord. Ann started taking my sons to church on Sundays, but she continued to faithfully visit me on Saturdays.

The church welcomed my family with open arms. As Christmas approached, I began to pray that God would provide a good Christmas for my sons—something I had never given them. Before I went to prison, I was so strung out on drugs that I never paid much attention to Christmas.

My sons were in the church Christmas play that year. Ann and her sister took them to the church for rehearsal and stayed inside to watch. I called Ann after rehearsal to see how it went. Her voice sounded excited and amazed at the same time, "You won't believe this!" she said. I asked, "What happened?" She told me that when she went to the car after rehearsal the church had filled her car with gifts for her and my sons—clothes and nice toys, including bicycles and basketballs. There were so many gifts they weren't even able to get in the car!

A scripture card attached to one of the bicycles read, "For God so loved the world that He gave His only begotten Son, that whosoever believeth in Him should not perish, but have everlasting life." (John 3: 16) and "But seek ye first the Kingdom of God and His righteousness, and all these things shall be added unto you." (Matthew 6:33) "Wow," I exclaimed, as I remembered: Matthew 6:33 was the scripture God had given me the morning of my sentencing. After the judge gave me eighty years, I felt God had let me down. I told my sister-in-law to tell Ann to read that scripture because it hadn't done anything for me, but maybe it would do something for her. I was reminded that all God's promises come to pass—not always in our timing, but in God's perfect time.

In 1988, when God began to deal with me about my education and how I would provide for my family when I got out of prison, I had attended classes to get my GED and took horticulture classes through Vo-Tech. Later, I enrolled in business college when it became available to me. It was through a young teacher, inexperienced with prison life, that Satan began a chain of events that caused a "kingpin" of a prison drug ring to rise up against me.

Our first test was the second or third week of class. After everyone completed their test, the teacher took up the papers, and then gave each of us a test to grade. The teacher read the correct answers and we were to put a check mark by any wrong answers. Then we wrote our names on the test paper and gave it back to the person who had filled it out. The test paper I graded had only two correct answers on the entire test. I didn't know the person whose name was on my paper, but I found him, walked across the room, handed the test paper to him, and started to walk away. Vile, filthy language exploded behind me. I grabbed my books and started down the hall. His evil roar followed me as I crossed the prison yard. He was calling me every name in the book, angry because I didn't cheat for him and correct his answers.

I stopped at the property room and picked up something, but he waited for me, cursing the entire time. He was a big, muscled guy, about 6'2", and he was following me to jump me. I began to pray silently, "God, what do I need to do?" The Lord told me to walk back over to him with boldness, tell him my name, tell him I am a Christian, tell him I am trying to live a Godly life and would not cheat for him on a test. Although I was shaking on the inside, I walked over to him with the boldness God gave me. He got right in my face cursing and threatening me. I knew he wanted to break my jaw. I repeated what God told me to tell him, turned, and walked away. He followed me for a few more feet, cursing and spewing vile, evil threats. Finally, he stopped following me. I walked to my cell thanking God for His guardian angels.

The more I learned about the inmate, the more fear started to grip me. As well as being a leader of a prison drug ring, he had a reputation for beating, stabbing, and bullying inmates and causing havoc in the prison. I didn't know who he was because I didn't hang around with that type of person any longer. I remembered what the atheist inmate had told me: "One day you'll have to put down your Bible and prove you are a man." I fell to my knees, "God, what do I do?" God told me that I never had to worry about defending myself unless someone put their hands on me. If they touched me, then I had the right or freedom to do what I had to do to survive.

For the next three weeks, the drug leader stared holes through me. I seemed to run into him everywhere—in business college classes, at the chow hall, on the ball field. His face snarled like a devil every time he saw me. It was obvious he wanted to attack me, but I believe in my heart that the angels of God were holding this guy back from jumping me. I never flinched or blinked when he stared, but on the inside fear gripped me. I began to pray, "God, please remove him from my life!" After three to four weeks, the guy disappeared from the prison yard. I knew the situation had been a snare of the devil; but by seeking God and obeying His voice, I had overcome Satan's evil plan to destroy me or to cause me to react in such a way that would stop the miracle God was about to bring into my life.

CHAPTER 5

I could hardly believe my eyes, but there it was—my name on the parole docket. *This must be a mistake*, I thought. *The counselors said the earliest date I could possibly come up for parole is February of 1997. This is February of 1990!* Since it was my second time in prison, I was told that I would be required to serve one third of my thirty-year sentence before I would even have a chance at a parole.

I looked down at my name again. *Surely*, I thought, *there isn't another Dixie Pebworth in the Oklahoma prison system.* I decided not to let myself get too excited until I could check this out. No one could tell me how my name appeared on the parole docket. I talked to my case manager, my counselor, and even asked the parole investigator. They all told me the same thing—they didn't know. But I knew. It was God working supernaturally on my behalf.

I immediately began writing a letter to send to all the parole board members. I told them what I was doing: that I had gone to school in prison and received my GED; that I had taken horticulture classes; that I was enrolled in business college; how I had changed my life and didn't want to be the same person that I was when I came to prison; what my goals were and what I was planning to do when I was released. The board voted unanimously to parole me from my thirty-year sentence to my forty-year sentence. It was an awesome day. I was so humbled; I kept thinking, *Who am I to deserve such goodness from the almighty God?*

God had done so many miracles in my life since I gave my heart to him in the Oklahoma County jail. God had answered my prayers to provide for my family; He had filled my mouth with water to quench the "cotton mouth" effects of marijuana; and He delivered me from drugs. He gave me a contact visit with my wife and, in the past year, He had restored our relationship. Now, He had given me a parole from a thirty-year sentence in only two and a half years.

I thought about how Satan had turned the leader of a prison drug ring against me. If I had reacted to his threats and gotten into a fight with him, I might not have received my parole. But God directed me through His still, small voice and protected me through that situation. I got down on my knees in my cell and poured out my heart of love and thankfulness to God for his goodness and mercy. The Holy Spirit reminded me of Matthew 6:33: "But seek ye first the Kingdom of God and His righteousness, and all these things shall be added unto you." As I obeyed God's Word and learned to know His voice, He added His blessings to my life.

I began serving my second sentence of forty years in 1990. I still had an appeal working in the appellate courts, but due to such a large number of cases pending, it could be several more years before there was a ruling. During this time, I also completed my three-year course and received a diploma from Rhema Bible Training Center. At the same time, I took several theology courses through Oklahoma Baptist University. I had a driving hunger to know more about God.

I was doing everything I knew to do to improve myself spiritually and mentally, but God began to deal with me about my physical body. He showed me that we are three parts—spirit, soul, and body—and that he wanted all three parts in 100% shape. When I went to prison I was smoking two packs of cigarettes a day, smoking marijuana, and using cocaine and meth. I could only run a few feet before I started coughing and hacking.

God delivered me from cigarettes in 1989 while I was in prison. I had tried to quit smoking several times, but wasn't successful. One morning God told me to put my foot on the cigarette pack. I pictured a combat boot coming down and breaking this big cigarette. I went all that day without a desire to smoke. At the end of the day, as I walked back to my cell, an inmate with a cigarette in his hand walked over to me. As he talked, I didn't hear a thing he said—all I could do was watch that cigarette going back and forth as he moved his hands.

James 1:2–4 came to my mind, "My brethren, count it all joy when ye fall into divers temptations, knowing this: that the trying of your faith worketh patience. But let patience have her perfect work, that ye may be perfect and entire, lacking nothing." I quoted that scripture in my mind several times while I stood there. I never thought about smoking again after that day.

Now, God was leading me to take another step in taking care of my body. A friend I had met in prison challenged me to start working out. He had been watching me in prison as I walked back and forth to the chapel services and lived my life for God. He eventually started going to church with me. He was a big muscular guy who lifted weights and he noticed that I jogged but never worked out in the gym. He started telling the other inmates that I was going to work out with him with weights. At that time, I hadn't agreed to working out with weights, but I wasn't about to back down from the challenge. Those first two weeks, every muscle in my body ached. He worked me so hard, I was too sore to put on my clothes without help. I kept working out, and after two weeks the pain and soreness subsided. After six months, I was stronger than he was; now the laugh was on him. By the time I was released from prison, I could bench press 400 lbs. and run five miles without breathing hard.

God continued to develop me in the areas where I needed to grow to fulfill His purpose in my life. At the time, I didn't fully know His purpose for me, but as I look back I can see that God used my prison time as a training ground. In prison, other people are always watching you. Every day they saw me carrying my Bible across the prison yard and saw that I was filled with peace and joy. Frequently an inmate would come to my cell and ask for prayer or ask me questions about a scripture in the Bible. I enjoyed these special times of ministry to the other inmates; God's presence was always there in that cell with us, for His Word says that where two or three are gathered together in His name, He will be with them. (Matthew 18:20)

In 1991, I was chosen with a group of seven other inmates to speak to kids through a program called "Straight Talk," which was modeled after a program called "Scared Straight." A deputy sheriff in Tulsa brought in kids from Gilcrease and Monroe middle schools. Both schools were known for drugs, gangs, and fights. We usually had thirty to forty kids in each class, and the classes were held three days a week with a different group every day until the entire school had been through the program.

When the kids walked in, as a sort of shock treatment, we began role playing scenarios commonly encountered in prison. If a kid tried to come across as tough or non-responsive, we would get in their face to tear down the wall so we could get through to them. We wanted them to quit being "tough" and realize the truth—there were horrors ahead of them if they continued their downward spirals. Once the walls came down, we'd sit and talk to the kids about prison life.

One of the inmates shared about the time he killed someone and the nightmare of watching them die. Then judgment fell on him. Just like he had shown no mercy to the person he killed, he was shown no mercy in the courtroom.

I wanted the kids to know how I felt seeing my wife weeping and clutching my young son in the courtroom when I was sentenced to eighty years. I wanted them to understand that I felt like I was attending my own funeral as I stood in that courtroom mourning with my family. I wanted them to feel my heartbreak when I watched my wife and sons walk out of the visitation room without me knowing if I'd ever go home with them again.

We talked about the madness of prison life—the horror of seeing another inmate stabbed to death, raped, or beat down. We tried to make the kids understand the oppression of living every day in a negative, cruel atmosphere that smothered any hope you had of making it out alive. No matter how tough an inmate appears to be on the outside, at night when they lay their head on a pillow, tears fill their eyes. The torment of prison life is overwhelming—even to the most hardened criminal.

We explained that prison is like a city inside a fence. It has its own currency. Back then, it was cigarettes, Little Debbie cakes, and soda pop. It was a bartering system with stores set up where you could buy, sell, and trade. There was drug use and drug dealing. There were homemade knives and constant madness with gang wars and fights. We were told every day what to wear, what to do, what time to get up, what you could eat, and what time to go to bed.

We had a board that displayed knives, called shanks, that were made in prison by inmates, along with pictures of people killed in prison by these knives. One of the pictures showed an inmate with a line wrapped around his neck. The death was ruled a suicide, but the inmates knew someone had killed him. One of my inmate friends had been killed in prison. He was the orderly for the day and had cleaned up the cigarette butts on the sidewalk. Another inmate walked behind him and threw down another cigarette butt. My friend and the other inmate got into an argument and made an agreement to meet behind the gym at night. My friend went alone to meet him, but the other inmate brought two to three other guys with him. They stabbed my friend twenty times and killed him over a cigarette butt. Another young man, age twenty-two, was killed over a hamburger that wasn't even real meat—just a soy burger. Another convict grabbed a shank and stabbed the young man in the heart.

I was allowed to share my own beliefs with the kids and talk about my experience with Jesus Christ, but I was not allowed to give an altar call. As I look back, I realize that this was the beginning of God training me to be a preacher. God used me to captivate these young hearts and minds and also used my testimony to touch the other inmates in our Straight Talk group. One of the inmates, a hardcore gang leader from LA, told me, "Man, you are getting to me." I said, "That's good." He was later saved and went to church with me.

Straight Talk made a lasting impact on the kids. Most of these children grew up in broken homes and many of their parents were in prison. There's so much falseness in this world and so much on television that glorifies the darkness of sex, sin, drugs, alcohol, guns, and power struggles. Television and movies cloud young minds, but the truth is these things only bring destruction. They take away your babies, your spouses, and your life; they destroy you from the inside out. When these kids saw tough men who could bench press 400 lbs. telling them the truth with tears rolling down their faces, it made an impact on their lives and the school.

During the program, the deputy sheriff who brought the kids asked me, "What are you going to do when you get out?" At first, I thought he was crazy to ask me such a question. I thought he hadn't been listening—didn't he understand that I had been sentenced to eighty years? I replied, "I've been sentenced to eighty years. I don't know if I'll ever get out of prison alive." He looked at me and said, "No, someday you'll get out. With your heart, the way you are, and the way you carry yourself, someday you'll get out. So again—what are you going to do when you get out?" I told him, "I don't know what I'll do, but I know one thing I don't want to do—I don't want to go back to Oklahoma City."

He asked me if I'd ever considered Tulsa. I told him my wife had attempted to move to Tulsa so she would be closer to the prison but hadn't been able to find a job that would support her and two children. He gave me his business card and said, "Here, have her call me." Obviously, this was something he wasn't supposed to do. Again, the favor of God was present.

Ann had an interview in Tulsa on a Friday and then drove to the prison to see me. By the time she arrived for our visit, the lady who interviewed her was calling her at the prison to offer her the position. The starting pay was $10 an hour, which was very good at that time, with a pay increase in thirty days. That was the first time I viewed the law enforcement agencies as something other than enemies.

After I had been at Conner prison for four and a half years, construction began on a minimum security facility to be built outside the fence of the main prison. I began praying that I would be allowed to move out to the minimum security prison when it was completed. I went to see my case manager, who told me there was no way I would be allowed to go out to minimum security. The rules required twenty years or less to serve and a nonviolent crime. I continued praying, "God, my life is in your hands and you are in control." I held on to God's promise in Matthew 7:7, "Ask, and it shall be given you; seek, and ye shall find; knock, and it shall be opened unto you." One week after the minimum security facility was opened, a guard came to me and said, "Get your bunk and junk. You are going out to minimum." Everyone was amazed; they kept saying they didn't understand why I was allowed to go the minimum facility. I just smiled and said, "Well, praise God!"

I had not been outside that prison fence for four and a half years except for my brief stay at the county jail at Plattsmouth, Nebraska. I was so thankful to walk past that fence and leave all that barbed wire, gang wars, and madness behind me. I was excited to think that I would have more freedom in family visitations. Since I had studied horticulture, I was chosen to do the landscaping at the warden's house and outside the prison.

It didn't take me very long to discover that there wasn't anything for the inmates in the minimum facility to do—no softball field, no gym, no weights to lift, and no church services because the facility was so new. I had grown accustomed to a church service being available every night. For the past three years, I had been the president of the choir inside the fence. My job was to keep unity and peace. I was also the overseer of special events. We had a great body of believers on the inside and a choir of men to sing praises to God. I really missed them.

I said, "God, I don't like it out here. I want to go back." God reminded me that I had asked to go to minimum security. I replied, "God, there are no church services out here." He said, "Start one." I said, "God. They won't let an inmate supervise a church service." He said, "How do you know if you don't ask?" I went to the unit manager and told her I wanted to start a church service. She said, "When?" I said, "Thursday nights at 7:00 p.m." She asked, "Where?" I replied, "The chow hall." To my amazement she said, "Okay." So now, I had to find people who wanted to go to church. I started walking around the facility inviting people to our first service. God taught me to do all things with diligence and to do it to the best of my ability as He continued to prepare me to fulfill His purpose for my life.

I was grateful to have a Thursday night service, but I still missed the choir, a group of men with whom I could sing praises to God. I went back to the unit manager and asked if we could start a choir. She asked me when and where. I told her Monday and Tuesday evenings in the chow hall. Again, she said, "Okay." The hard part was to find men who wanted to sing in a choir. But within three months, we had twelve men in the choir and we added a Sunday morning service. I taught the Thursday night Bible study for the remainder of my time in prison. It was during this time that I began to realize that God had a pastoral calling on my life.

I could see that Ann was getting tired from the pressure of having to raise two boys alone, now six and eight. Struggling with finances to make ends meet, the boys' school activities, a full time job, and coming to the prison every weekend were draining her. To her, our visits had become more of a duty instead of a time to enjoy each other. In the spring of 1993, I suggested she come to the prison less often to take some pressure off her. But she kept coming as often as she could, only missing a couple of weekends. She hadn't found a church where she felt like she fit in after she moved to Tulsa. After a while, she gave up and stopped going to church.

Ann learned that the Court of Criminal Appeals would rule on my case on June 23, 1993. On June 24, she called the appeals office and she was told that Count Three of my sentence had been "vacated and dismissed." She thought Count Three was my ten-year sentence, but that I still had the forty-year sentence to complete. She couldn't take the pressure any longer and had a nervous breakdown.

I called Ann around June 28 to find out if she was coming to the prison on the Fourth of July, or whether she had decided to spend the day with her family in Oklahoma City. When she answered the phone, she was crying. I asked her what was wrong. She told me the court had ruled on my case and vacated Count Three, which she said had to be the ten-year sentence. I said, "Not necessarily." I was thinking back to my jury trial, *Count Two was 'Not Guilty' and Count Three was the possession of a weapon while in commission of a felony, for which I received forty years.* Ann insisted Count Three was the ten-year sentence and that I would have to spend at least another five to six years in prison even with my "good time," which is commonly referred to as time off for good behavior. Ann was distraught. She kept saying she couldn't take it anymore and she couldn't wait any longer. I told her Count Three was not the ten-year sentence. She said, "Yes, it is!" We got into an argument and were both mad when we hung up the phone.

After that, Ann refused to answer my phone calls. She had met a guy at a picnic a few months prior and had become friends with him. He had a career, made good money, and had a secure, comfortable life—things that are very important to a woman. After her breakdown, she moved in with him.

It was two to three weeks later before I learned what the Court of Criminal Appeals had ruled. My cell mate enjoyed spending time in the law library. About the middle of July, he rushed into the cell waiving a sheet of paper that read, "Pebworth vs State." The appellate court had vacated and dismissed Count Three which was my forty-year sentence.

I rushed to the phone and called Ann, but she had forwarded her phone to the man's house where she was now living. I slammed down the phone when the man answered. Anger welled up inside me, forcing out the peace of God that had become my daily companion.

The next couple of weeks were tormenting. I tried to pray but my anger blocked me from hearing God's voice and experiencing His peace. Satan had come again to "kill, steal and destroy." (John 10:10) This time he had come to destroy my testimony.

I was hurt, I was sad, and I was angry at Satan and my wife. I certainly wasn't prepared for the package I would soon receive in the prison mail.

CHAPTER 6

I held the package in my hands for a few minutes, staring, not sure I wanted to know what was inside. I had just picked up my mail and received a package from my wife. When I opened it, I learned that my wife had sent me divorce papers.

I was deeply hurt, and at the same time, I was furious as the contents of the package really sank in. How could she do this—now—when I would soon receive my notice of the day I would be set free? How could she take my sons from me—now? Every night before I went to bed, I had prayed for my freedom and now God had answered my prayers. In just weeks or at most a few months, I could go home. But, now, I didn't have a home.

My ego took over. "Well, if that's what she wants—that's what she'll get," I angrily said aloud. I immediately took the papers to the administrative office, signed them, and had them notarized. Then I went back to my cell, put stamps on the package and started to storm out of the cell to mail them. My cell mate was a little guy, but he stepped in front of me and started begging me to let him "say just one thing." At that time, I was bench pressing 400 lbs. and he certainly could not have prevented me from walking through that door. But he just kept begging until I said, "Okay!" He asked, "Is this really what you want?" I said, "No." He replied, "Then, why give it to her?"

In anger, I threw the package across the cell, then crawled in my bed and stayed there for four days—reading the Bible, crying, and praying. My cell mate began to worry about me because I refused to eat for those four days. I was talking to God, but the devil was talking to me. "I've destroyed your testimony! You just thought you were going to walk out of here and tell the world how God gave everything back to you!" The devil tried to set me up and make me run—to escape and go after my wife. Thank God for spiritual men of God who came to prison to minister. My anger and self-pity blocked me from hearing God's still, small voice; I desperately needed the spiritual counsel of a brother in Christ.

One minister in particular really helped me; it was Pastor Ricky who had led my wife to the Lord. Pastor Ricky came to the prison an hour early for chapel to visit with me in the chow hall prior to the service. He asked me if I knew what James 4:7 says. I repeated it back to him, "Submit yourselves therefore to God. Resist the devil, and he will flee from you." Pastor Ricky encouraged me, "This is just an attack of the devil to destroy your testimony." I said, "No, you don't understand. My wife has moved in with another guy, she won't answer my phone calls, she won't come see me, and she's sent divorce papers. She has destroyed my testimony!"

Pastor Ricky said, "No, you don't understand James 4:7." I said, "No. You don't understand." I told him again what my wife was doing. Pastor Ricky said again, "What does James 4:7 say? You are not doing what it says." I said, "Yes, I am." He said, "No, you are not! Every time you tell me the story of what she's doing, you're giving the devil power over your life. Stop looking at what the devil's doing, start resisting him and submit yourself to God." Finally, I understood what Pastor Ricky was saying. I hadn't been to a church service or the choir for the past week—I was too angry and too busy feeling sorry for myself. The first thing I did was to stop giving the devil power over my life by repeating what my wife was doing at that time. Then I submitted myself to God by doing the things God had taught me to do when I gave my life to Him in the county jail—seeking God, praying, reading the Bible, and witnessing.

I continued to try to reach Ann to let her know that it was my forty-year sentence that had been vacated and dismissed and that I would soon be free. Even when she learned that it was my forty-year sentence, she didn't call or come see me because she felt that I wouldn't be able to forgive her. Finally, Ann came to see me in September. We hadn't spoken since the end of June.

At the time of Ann's visit, she was still living with the other guy. We sat in the visiting room and talked, both of us crying much of the time. We knew God had worked miracles to set me free. Ann said she knew I wouldn't be able to forgive her but I assured her I could and already had. She asked me where I would go to serve my parole. I told her I supposed I would go back to Oklahoma City and stay with my mom and dad since she was with someone else.

Ann returned to visit me the following week. She said she wanted to try to make it work for us, although she still felt that I could not forgive her. I explained to her that when you submit yourself to God, you do what God says in His Word. The Bible says that if God has forgiven us, we must forgive others and let go of all bitterness, anger, and wrath. Ann told me she had continued to pay rent on her apartment even though she wasn't living there and that she had moved back into her apartment. Obeying God's Word had brought another miracle into my life. I submitted myself to God; resisted the devil; and he fled from me. (James 4:7)

In October 1993 (four months after my appeal had been granted), I received notice that my discharge date would be January 24, 1994. I remember thinking, *I'm really going to be free. It's no longer a prayer and a confession—I will really be free!* When my forty-year sentence was vacated and dismissed, the three and a half years I had served on the forty-year sentence was applied to my ten-year sentence plus my "good time." For every thirty days of good behavior, an inmate was given forty-four days off the back of their sentence. My good time had accumulated to several years by now; my ten-year sentence would be "discharged," meaning served in full, in three more months.

I spent the last three months of my prison term in a work release center in McAlester, Oklahoma, where I was allowed to do lawn work on a golf course. In the work release program, I was allowed to go outside the facility to church. My wife drove down every weekend, and we went to church together.

As my discharge date approached, I expected to receive paperwork telling me when and where to report for my parole, but nothing was ever said to me about a parole. On the day of my discharge, I became apprehensive—I was afraid I was being set up and that when I didn't report for my parole, I would be sent back to prison. I asked the case manager where I needed to report. She said, "What are you talking about? You are being discharged." I replied, "Yes, but I have a parole from my thirty-year sentence, and I want to know where to go. I don't want to have to come back here." The case manager went back to the office and soon returned with a paper in her hand. She said, "I don't know what you are talking about, but here is the paper stating you are free. As long as you have this paper, there is nothing anyone can do to you." "Wow," I said, "I am a free man!"

I walked out of prison with Ann on January 24, 1994, after serving six years, three months, and seventeen days of an eighty-year sentence. "Thank you, God!" I muttered as I took a deep breath and looked up at the beautiful blue sky. After putting my things in the trunk of the car, Ann and I joined hands and made a vow to each other that from that day forward nothing in the past would ever be brought up again except to help someone else. We prayed together, then drove away from the prison, never looking back.

The first thing out of Ann's mouth as we drove away was to ask, "Where do you have to go to report for parole?" I said, "I don't have parole." She said, "Yes, you do." I said, "No, I don't." She gave me a stern glance and repeated, "You've got parole!" I showed her the paperwork and proudly announced, "They said they don't know anything about a parole for me and as long as I have this paper, they can't do anything to me."

I was excited that I did not have the restraints of a parole, but at the same time I was apprehensive. I knew Satan and some of my old friends would try to tempt me to return to my old lifestyle. At that time, I felt I needed the control of a parole; Ann definitely felt I needed supervision. She was afraid I would return to a life of drugs.

Before we arrived at our apartment in Tulsa, Ann took me to a buffet for lunch. To walk out of a prison chow hall to rows of assorted meats, vegetable dishes, fruits, desserts, soups, and breads caught me off guard. For six years, a plate of prison food had been shoved at me. I felt confused and awkward—I just wanted to sit down. Ann saw my confusion and came to my rescue.

We came home to Ann's one-bedroom apartment, but that was okay with me. It was a lot bigger than my prison cell! Her furniture was a broken down dining room table, a loveseat, a set of bunk beds for our sons, and a mattress and box springs on the floor where she slept. She was still using the color console TV I bought before I went to prison and the entertainment center I had built. She was a single mom raising two kids and barely getting along.

I couldn't wait to surprise my sons, nine-year-old Little Dixie and seven-year-old Cory, when they came home from school. We hadn't told them I'd be coming home that day. God had taught me the importance of the words we speak when we are standing in faith for our prayers to be answered. I had asked God what I should say when people asked how long I had to serve in prison. God told me to say, "Man says I have eighty years; but God says I will soon be free." So when my sons asked when I would be coming home, we would tell them "soon." They had waited so long.

Finally, it was time for the boys to come home from school. I hid in the bedroom until they slammed the door and I heard them drop their books on the floor. When I walked around the corner, they jumped on me. We had so much fun just wrestling and rolling around in the floor. I was so blessed to be back with my family.

That night, I pulled the mattress and box springs out of the bedroom where my sons slept—something my boys couldn't understand. They kept asking why we couldn't all sleep in the same room.

The past summer, Ann's uncle had given white rats to each of the boys, and Ann's mother had let them keep the rats for pets. At first, Ann told them they couldn't bring their pets home with them, but after much begging she conceded. One of the pet rats had gotten away two or three days prior to me coming home and was still loose in the apartment. I didn't get much sleep that night with a rat on the loose and me sleeping on the floor. The rat kept coming out from behind the dishwasher. I'd jump up and he would run behind it again. The rat and I repeated this scenario several times during the night. The boys and Ann had grown accustomed to the rats and laughed at me.

The next night, I waited up for the rat. I dumped the boy's toys out of a plastic tub and left the dining room light on, so I could see him when he came out. For fifteen minutes, I stood vigil trying not to move a muscle, my right hand resting on the plastic tub I had leaned on the kitchen countertop. I had him this time! Slamming the plastic tub over him and securing it with a weight, I left him till morning and got some sleep.

The next morning, I told the boys they could no longer let their rats run loose in the house. The first time their grandmother came to visit, I put the caged rats in her car and told the boys we would get them a different pet. My sons are adults now, but they still remember the rat story.

Ann graciously told me to take a couple weeks to rest and unwind, and then I could look for a job. I spent the first three days cleaning, praising God, inviting Him into our home, and praying for my family. At the end of the third day, Ann came home from work and told me she had found a job for me—so much for the two weeks off! Ann was an accountant for a trucking company at the airport. She had told her boss about me, and he said he might give me a chance when I got out of prison. Her boss had signed a contract to load and unload 1,000 lb. containers into cargo airplanes at the Tulsa International Airport. When she told him I was home, he asked to have me come in the next day.

When I was discharged from prison, I was in good shape mentally, spiritually, and physically. He took one look at me and said, "You're hired." He sent me to the airport security office to get a badge. When I filled out the paperwork, I told the truth about my felony record. The security officer looked at my application and said, "I can't give you a badge." I replied, "I told the owner of the company, but he said he could get a badge for whoever he wanted, so you can call him." The owner of the company told the officer, "Look, I'll hire who I want to hire. Give him a badge." The officer hung up and gave me a badge that gave me entrance to the runway of an international airport. "Well, praise God," I responded. God had given me favor once again. Within twelve months, I was promoted to foreman and in charge of loading and unloading the planes.

My first Sunday out of prison, I woke up early and got dressed for church. I then woke up my sons and got them dressed. Together, we woke up my wife and told her we were going to church and asked if she wanted to go with us. She did! We drove to Edmond, Oklahoma, to attend the services of Pastor Ricky's church. He was my spiritual father who had led my wife to the Lord and whose church had given my family such a nice Christmas five years previously. I wanted to personally thank the church for taking my family in and loving them. Pastor Ricky is also the one who had helped me understand the meaning of James 4:7 (submit yourselves therefore to God; resist the devil, and he will flee from you).

After the service, I took my family to visit my adoptive parents in Oklahoma City. Shortly after we arrived at my parents' house, there was a knock at the door. Donnie, a neighborhood friend since before kindergarten, had heard I was out of prison and came by to see "if I was for real." I shared the gospel with Donnie for two hours and told him all that God had done in my life. Finally he said, "Okay, it's real. I'll see you later." I never heard from him again.

When I was at Conner prison in 1989, a former friend I had looked up to at the age of fourteen was sent to Conner to spend the last three months of his prison term. He was still using drugs in prison and had tried on several occasions to get me high with him. I always refused the drugs, but I would witness to him and invite him to the chapel services. When he was released from prison, he told everyone I had become a Jesus freak. Although he never went to church with me in prison, he later gave his life to the Lord.

Ann and I visited some churches in the Tulsa area but were not comfortable in any of them. So for the next three months we drove to Edmond every Sunday to Pastor Ricky's church.

I knew my family would get the love and spiritual food we needed there.

Over the next few months, Satan threw several hurdles at us, trying to discourage us and drive me back to the world of drugs that had previously destroyed me from the inside out. I worked a split shift so it was a necessity to have two cars. The cost to get my driver's license back was $900, and I had to wait until I completed a DUI school prior to reinstating my license even though I had completed the drug classes in prison. My dad bought a 1977 Monte Carlo for me. He said, "Son, I wasn't able to buy a car for you when you were sixteen. But you're doing good now and I want to buy you a car." I was so blessed. The car was seventeen years old, but it was very special to me.

Shortly after I was discharged from prison, I was contacted by the child support bureau to repay the child support payments my first wife had collected on our daughter while I was in prison; I owed $8,000 in back pay. Ann and I worked hard to try to make ends meet, but there were weeks we just couldn't stretch our money far enough.

Satan began to plague me. "You know you can make the money you need by selling drugs. Just call your old friends in Oklahoma City and let them know you're back in business." Satan was relentless. "In a day, you could make more money selling drugs than you make now in a week. You could even pay tithes on the money you make and help the church." Satan had come again to "kill, steal, and destroy." But I stood my ground, quoting Ephesians 6:16, "Above all, taking the shield of faith, wherewith ye shall be able to quench all the fiery darts of the wicked." As I meditated in that scripture, my faith was strengthened: I knew God would provide financially for us. I wanted nothing to do with drugs ever again in my life.

About six months after I got out of prison, Satan laid a trap to try to put me back in jail. My oldest son had a nice mountain bike that had been stolen from our apartment complex. One Saturday he came running upstairs to our apartment yelling, "Dad, I found my bike. This girl is riding it down the street." I grabbed my keys and we jumped in the car. I drove past the girl and stopped. I asked my son how he knew it was his bike, and he began showing me all the scratches he had put on the bike and what he had done to cause the damage. I asked the girl where she got the bike. She said, "I bought it." I said, "No, this is my son's bike, and it was stolen about a week ago. My son can tell you every scratch and dent on this bike and how it happened." She started to ride away, but I grabbed the back of the tire and held it. She started screaming, "Rape! Call the police!" I thought, *Oh my God! What have I gotten myself into?* I let go of the tire and she crossed the street and rode back to a pharmacy a block away. When I pulled into the parking lot behind her, she rode the bike through the door past the cash register and started screaming at the top of her lungs, "He's trying to attack me! Somebody call the police!" When I saw what she was doing, I was terrified. I told my son to get in the car, and I drove off. My son yelled, "Dad, where are you going?" I said, "I don't know."

The Spirit of God began to warn me, "Turn the car around and go back. If you don't, you'll have a warrant for your arrest." I drove back to the pharmacy and went inside. The girl began screaming again. I asked the cashier to call the police. He said he had already called the police and asked me to wait outside.

Soon, three squad cars arrived. I told the policeman that my son's bike had been stolen and this girl had his bike. He asked me if I had a serial number for the bike on me. I told him no. He asked for a receipt. I didn't have that either. Then he asked how I knew it was my son's bike. I told him my son could describe every scratch and dent on the bike and how it got there and where he was when the accident happened.

The policeman took my son aside and talked to him. My son accurately described every scratch on the bike. The policeman came back to me and said, "This is your son's bike all right. But I can't do anything about it. She has a receipt in her pocket from Toys R Us. I asked how much the receipt was for. He said, "$75." I said, "But this is a $200 bike!" The policeman ignored me and started writing out a ticket with a charge of assault and battery against me.

CHAPTER 7

———

I dreaded telling Ann about the assault and battery charge. *What else is going to happen?* I thought. *How will we ever afford an attorney?* I was beginning to wear down physically and emotionally; we desperately needed relief from Satan's relentless attacks.

Since there was no money in our budget for an attorney, I represented myself in the courtroom. The DA recommended a year in the county jail. "But I didn't touch her!" I objected. "I held the back bicycle tire to keep her from riding away on my son's stolen bicycle." The judge rescheduled the hearing and told me to get an attorney.

I had only been out of prison six months. I couldn't bear the thought of going back to jail for a year! It would destroy my family and my testimony. Surely, God could use me in ministry on the outside. Surely He didn't want me to go back to jail.

The cost of the attorney was $5,000—over a $200 bike! I told my son if his bike was ever stolen again, we wouldn't try to recover the bike, we'd just buy him a new one. I was given a deferred sentence for a misdemeanor of assault and battery and told to stay away from the victim. Even though I hadn't touched her, the court ruled that I "detained" her by grabbing the bicycle wheel when she tried to ride off on my son's bike.

As I left the courtroom, I shuddered at the thought, *If I had been given parole when I was discharged from prison, I might not be walking out of this courtroom right now. I might be in handcuffs on my way back to Conner.* God, in His wisdom, looked ahead and protected me. I was and still am so grateful. We serve a good God—a God of love.

We were soon able to move out of the one-bedroom apartment into a three-bedroom house in a different neighborhood and life began to be good. In February 1995—a little over a year after I had been released from prison—I answered the phone and a woman's voice said, "Would you like to have your daughter?" At first, I was stunned but then I recognized the voice to be that of my ex-wife. She was going into the military and could not take our daughter with her initially. "Sure," I said. In prison, I had asked God to restore the relationship between me and my daughter.

I left my first wife because she insisted that I stop using drugs. After the divorce, she moved out of state with my three-year-old daughter, Misty. While I was in prison, I told Ann that I hadn't seen my daughter for ten years, but I had asked God to reunite us and give me an opportunity to be a father to her.

Ann located my ex-wife and brought my daughter to prison to visit me. We spent about eight hours in the visiting room, playing games and talking. At the end of the visit, Misty looked at me and said, "You're nothing like what Mama says you are." I looked at her with a big smile and replied, "Look, you see what I am today. What your mom has probably told you was true back then, but because of my born-again experience with God and what He has done in my life, I am who I am today."

My family quickly outgrew our little three-bedroom house. Misty came to live with us in March and later that year, our third son, JJ, was born. JJ was an answer to my prayer. While I was still in prison, Ann and I had a conversation about having more kids. She looked at me and said, "I'll never have any more kids!" I laughed because God had already told me that He would give me a son that I could raise because I had missed the early years with my first two sons. JJ was my son born out of season, and he was the one that I would get to take to his first day of school and coach his baseball team. I remember his first day of kindergarten. I walked him to his classroom with tears streaming down my face. I'm sure everyone thought I was a crybaby, but I was so blessed that God had given me another chance to be a father. JJ's full name is Joseph Jeremiah, which means, "God adds and God exalts."

By now, Ann and I had finally found a church in the Tulsa area where we felt comfortable. When I was first released from prison, we visited several churches in the Tulsa area including Victory Christian Center. I considered Billy Joe Daugherty one of my spiritual fathers because his teaching had been a blessing to me while I was in prison. We visited Victory the second

Sunday I was out of prison, but the size of the church was overwhelming to me—being fresh out of prison, I didn't like crowds. So for the first few months, we drove to Edmond to be in the services of Pastor Ricky's church where we were loved and accepted by the people.

After about ninety days, Pastor Ricky told me, "You know you need to find a church closer to home." I knew he was right. Soon after that, I received a phone call from one of my spiritual fathers who had faithfully come to the prison to minister. He lived in the Tulsa area and attended a church in West Tulsa. He told me they had a new pastor, and he wanted me to come to a service to meet him. Ann and I visited the church the next two Sundays. There were only forty people in attendance our first Sunday in a sanctuary with a seating capacity of five to six hundred, but we felt God's presence and felt that this was the church God would have us attend.

I was excited and got busy inviting people to church. I loved the people and I thought the people loved me. One day the pastor called me into his office and said, "You have to stop scaring the people." I blurted, "What? I'm not scaring people!" I used my hands as I talked to make a point. The pastor replied, "That's what I mean. Your voice and mannerisms scare the people." I quickly responded, "I'm not scaring people! I just learned not to mumble in prison. You talk straight and say what you mean." When I came out of prison, I was a big guy— muscled up from lifting weights and running. The people didn't yet know me, and my boldness was intimidating to them. The pastor was trying to help me and began to spend time coaching and fellowshipping with me.

After a few months, one of the Sunday School teachers asked me if I would like to take over his Sunday School class of couples under age forty. He was in his sixties and wanted to teach the older couples. I wanted to build a big Sunday School class, so I planned a fellowship on a Saturday night and invited four or five people to sing. I planned a feast fit for a king, and over a thirty-day period, I invited over one hundred people.

On the night of the fellowship, five people showed up; my wife and I were two of the five; one of the singers came and two people came to help prepare the food. I sat in the fellowship hall thinking to myself, *God, what's the use?" These people don't want You.* In prison, I was accustomed to having church every night. It was hard for me to understand why people on the outside didn't want to go to church more often. God showed me that you don't start something and expect a harvest right away. You've got to plow the ground; plant the seed; fertilize and water. For the next three years, I taught Sunday School to a class of eight to twenty people. I just kept sowing, plowing, and watering.

My spiritual father, Don Bailey, who had invited me to the church in 1994, was grooming me to take over his ministry at Conner prison when he died. He was in his seventies and knew his years on earth were numbered. In 1997, I was ordained as a minister and started going into the prisons to preach the gospel.

Soon, I was ministering to as many as two thousand inmates per week throughout prisons in Oklahoma. My bait to attract inmates to come to the services was my testimony of being delivered from an eighty-year prison sentence.

On October 12, 1997—my 10 year spiritual birthday—I was given the opportunity to share my testimony in the church service. The people were blessed and excited to hear how the Spirit of God was working—it brought life and hope to the church. That night the church took up an offering to start a fund for prison ministry.

I invited the choir from our church to sing at a "Setting the Captives Free" tent revival in a prison in Vinita, Oklahoma, on the Friday night I was scheduled to preach. Twenty-five choir members drove to Vinita to minister to the inmates. When I gave an altar call, men began to stream into the tent from the prison yard and join those inside the tent who came forward to give their lives to God. The tent was packed, and at least ninety inmates lined up across the front of the tent for prayer. With tears streaming down their faces, some of the choir members stopped singing to come down and help pray for the inmates.

The revival made an impact on the choir. They realized that God was moving in the prisons, and they saw it as a mission field. They wanted to know what they could do to help me and how we could help these people after they were released from prison. I was amazed by the change in the hearts of the choir members. I'd been praying for a way to help these inmates because many of them had nowhere to go except back to the place that had made them criminals.

Soon, we began taking vans to the pre-release centers on Sundays to bring inmates to church and serve them a meal before taking them back. My Sunday School class grew from twenty to one hundred people. Many of them continued to come to our church after they were released.

I gave the church members some simple advice: "When people come from the pre-release centers, love them and make them feel welcome, but don't take them to your home because you don't know them. If you want to provide a meal for them, take them to a restaurant." They asked how to love them. I told them to treat them the same way they treated me and my family when we started coming to the church.

As God's anointing increased in my life, Ann and I knew that God would eventually open the door for me to go into full-time ministry. We agreed that when the time was right, we would know it.

In 1998, I was working as the operations manager for Lampton Welding Supply and was bringing home $900 every two weeks. The area manager told me the company had to lay off two people and asked me who I wanted to let go. I had hired one of my friends, when he was released from prison, who had two daughters to support. He was doing a good job and I didn't want to let him go. Everyone under me was working out well and I didn't want to let any of them go. As I stood there looking at the area manager, I heard God's voice—the voice I had learned to hear and obey when I was in prison. The Spirit of God inside me said, "The time is now. The harvest is white." I cringed at the thought of leaving my job. Ann and I had agreed that we would know when it was time—was this the time?

God's voice grew stronger, "The harvest is white." I realized this was God's timing. I turned to my manager and said, "If you will give me two weeks paid vacation and my 401(k), I'll take a voluntary layoff." He was surprised but said, "I'll call the main office and get back to you with an answer." The answer was "yes." Now I had to tell my wife!

Before I talked to Ann, I went to the pastor of our church and told him I was ready to go into full-time ministry and was willing to be responsible for my own salary. I wanted the church to pay me $150 per week out of the prison ministry account, which had accumulated by now to about $3,000. As the prison ministry funds grew, my salary would be increased. The church board agreed to my offer.

When I told Ann about the days' events, she began to tell me all the reasons why I could not quit my job at that time. She cried when I told her I had already quit. She said that without my income of $900 every two weeks, we couldn't meet our budget. I asked her to go to our bedroom and pray until she heard from God, then come out and tell me what He said to her. If she did not agree that it was time to go into full-time ministry, I would look for another job. She was weeping when she came out of the bedroom. She said, "In my heart I know you are doing what God called you to do—but my head is telling me it won't work." She agreed to the arrangements I had made to begin full-time ministry, but she felt I had left her behind—a feeling Satan would later use in an attempt to destroy us.

I asked one of my spiritual fathers, Pastor Ricky, to meet with me. Excitedly, I began to tell him all the things I wanted to do. He finally interrupted me and said, "Dixie, ministry is not what is important." Puzzled, I replied, "What do you mean ministry is not important? Ministry is everything!" He repeated, "Ministry is not what's important. Ministry will always be here—there's always plenty of hurting people. But what is important is your relationship with God; without that relationship, there will be no ministry." I said, "Okay, I see that"—a lesson well learned as I would later find out.

One of the first outreaches I started in the church was a Friday night support group with a relaxed atmosphere. We had a band with uplifting praise and worship and a time for testimonies. I ended the service by preaching a sermon and giving an altar call. We were bringing in inmates from the local pre-release centers, and God's Spirit was moving in our services. We grew from thirty people on Friday nights to around two hundred consistently.

In 1998, we held a "Setting the Captives Free" revival at our church. I asked my spiritual father, Don Bailey, who had groomed me to take over his ministry at Conner prison, to come to a service to pray over me and anoint me with oil for a double portion of his anointing. Don was ill, and I went to his house to help his wife get him into a wheelchair and bring him to the service. It was the last church service Don was able to attend before he passed away.

In 1999, I invited my spiritual father Dave King, to a "Setting the Captives Free" revival service. Dave had started a Christian-based non-profit organization in 1983 to help people who were released from prison or wanted to be free from an addiction. His organization, Freedom Ranch, Inc., had seven programs in various locations. F.I.R.S.T. Wings of Freedom was a drug treatment program located in Tulsa for pregnant women and women with children. (F.I.R.S.T. is an acronym for Families In Recovery Staying Together.) I had shared with Dave that I wanted to start a housing program and recovery support for people transitioning from prison to society.

Dave asked me to attend the next board meeting of Freedom Ranch, Inc. and soon I was invited to be a board member. As I look back now, I see the hand of God leading and training me for the position I have today—the CEO of Freedom Ranch, Inc. Dave and I had similar visions—to restore people's lives and to make the organization self-sustaining by creating businesses that would support the ministry and create jobs for the people in our program.

After I had been on the board of Freedom Ranch for a little over a year, Dave asked me to meet with him. Dave handed me a ball of keys and said, "Here, start your housing program. But at first, I want you to start with just women and children." Dave told me I could use the first, third, and fourth floors of his building that had previously housed F.I.R.S.T. Wings of Freedom as well as the community kitchen in the basement. Satan had launched an attack on Freedom Ranch, Inc. over the past ten years, and due to finances, Dave was being forced to shut down several programs. He had not been financially able to make the mortgage payment on the building for over a year. The businessman who carried the note agreed that I could use the building rent free until all the apartments were filled. Then I would have to start paying rent, so Dave could make the mortgage payment. I had the keys, I had the vision—and suddenly I had fear. *This dream is really happening!* I thought. I felt small in comparison to this big responsibility. But as always, God began to work supernaturally to bring about His plan for my life.

The eighteen apartments were fully furnished but needed repairs to make them livable. My Sunday School class rallied to support me. The men helped me paint and make the repairs. Several women in the class volunteered to work with the women and children from twenty to forty hours a week. The women who lived in the apartments would be required to get jobs, pay a small amount of rent each month, and contribute a portion of their income to buy food that would be prepared for everyone in the community kitchen. We renamed the organization "New Beginnings Wings of Freedom" and took in a family as soon as the first apartment was ready.

As each apartment was finished, we filled it with homeless women coming out of prison, or drug treatment, or fleeing from domestic violence. Many of the women had children. We took them all in to keep the families together. Many times towards the end of the month, our food supply would run low. But God was faithful. Always, we would have a knock at the door and open it to find someone holding bags of food. No one ever went hungry.

I shared my testimony with every church that would open their doors to raise money for Wings of Freedom. Asbury United Methodist Church in Tulsa was a godsend to us, donating $6,000 the first year and $3,000 the second and third years through their missions program. In March of the first year, I received a $2,000 heating bill—it was a cold winter and our heat for the apartments was a boiler system that never shut off. I gasped when I saw the invoice from the gas company. I had no idea how I would pay $2,000. About three days later, we received exactly $2,000 in the mail from Asbury United Methodist Church. It didn't take a rocket scientist to figure out what God wanted us to do with the money. We paid the heating bill.

The Friday night service at the church continued to thrive for the next two years with people getting saved, healed, and delivered from addictions. With the exception of the pastor, I had a lot of support from the church staff, faithfully coming to help me on Friday nights with the music, prayer, counseling, and whatever needed to be done. The offerings on Friday night went into the prison ministry so the church was able to increase my weekly salary, which relieved the financial pressure for my family.

During the summer of 2000, the staff gathered for our weekly meeting with the pastor. The first thing out of the pastor's mouth was, "I want you to stop helping Dixie on Friday nights. Stop supporting him and start your own ministries." I felt like I had been slapped in the face. Sitting at the end of the table in full view of the other staff members, I tried not to show any emotion but my mind was whirling: *Why?* In my opinion, I had in no way, shape, or form threatened him or done anything to cause this. I'd even invited the pastor to preach on Friday nights, but he'd never accepted. The staff helped me voluntarily because they saw souls being saved and lives changed. They were all a blessing to me, and I loved them. As far as I knew, the staff loved me as well.

The pastor tried to explain: He told the staff he wanted them to stop feeding off my ministry and get their own ministry. He felt they were not answering "their" call, but that they were answering "my" call. I couldn't understand why he didn't think that saving souls and changing lives is everyone's call.

I didn't say anything in the meeting out of respect for the pastor as our leader, but I stayed behind after the staff was dismissed to talk to him privately. When we were alone, I spoke up. "I don't know what's going on, but what you just did is wrong. Here we are in the trenches winning souls for the kingdom of God and you've just divided your army and sent it in five different directions. You've crippled us." The pastor repeated the explanation he had given in the meeting—that he wanted everyone to get on with their own calling. He told me that I didn't understand now, but that I would understand later. I never did.

I left the meeting angry with my pastor and began to withdraw from him and he from me. Prior to the staff meeting, the pastor and I had constantly communicated. We never discussed what his sermon would be or what I would teach in Sunday School, but often his sermon would complete the lesson I had taught an hour earlier; we were kindred spirits. He had trained me and poured into my life for the seven years I had been in the church, and I admired him for that. But after his announcement in the staff meeting, I was unable to receive spiritually from him.

Over the next few months, God began to deal with me about resigning my position as associate pastor and leaving the church. I said, "But God, I love these people. I led many of them to the Lord, and I want to stay and minister to them." I didn't hear a voice from a burning bush, but I felt a wooing from the spirit of God to look around me. God showed me that there were 100,000 people in Tulsa that still needed to be saved, but my eyes were fixed on the two to three hundred that had already come into the fold.

In January 2001, Ann and I went to a cabin in the mountains for a few days to have some time together away from the pressures of ministry. An ice and snow storm kept us inside the cabin most of the time we were away. We had a lot of time to talk about the ministry, our future, and whether it was time to leave the church.

When we returned from our trip, the pastor hired my lifetime friend to be the youth minister in our church. I was excited. I cherished being able to serve God with a friend who had formerly followed the same life of crime I had followed but had since given his life to God. I reasoned, *What I'm feeling must not be God. He doesn't want me to leave.* The prison fund at the church had built up to $8,000 so I felt my salary was secure. I thought, *How can I put my family through another period of financial hardship?*

I made my decision. I would follow my head – not my heart. That decision began a heartbreaking series for me of making wrong choices. Although I couldn't see it coming at the time, I would wish many times over the next year that I had obeyed God and chosen His path for my life.

CHAPTER 8

━∞━

Having made the decision to stay at the church even though I felt God was leading me to resign, I jumped head first into trying to maintain the outreaches we had started. As associate pastor, I was also required to be in all the scheduled services of the church, even though the other staff members were no longer attending the inmate outreaches. The Friday night support group required many hours of preparation, study, and counseling. Wings of Freedom was requiring more and more of my time, with all eighteen apartments filled with women and children who had been homeless, or were coming off drugs, or had been recently released from prison.

On week nights, I took members from the Friday night support group to various prisons in Oklahoma to hold chapel services. On Saturdays, I went back into the prisons with an organization named Prison Invasion. We were allowed to go onto the prison yard, hand out tracts, and minister one on one. Then Saturday night, I would preach the prison chapel service, get home late, and get up early on Sunday to teach a Sunday School class of about one hundred at my church. Sunday nights, I ministered at Sac & Fox or Thunderbird Youth Academy, or I would go to a church to give my testimony to raise money for the prison ministry.

One night I had a dream: Ann and I were in a storm in a small boat about the size of the ski boats used on Oklahoma lakes. We were in the ocean, driving at full throttle across the white caps. Without warning, a tidal wave billowed in front of us and shot our small boat straight up in the air. As the boat came down, it nosedived into the ocean and never surfaced again. Ann and I were left thrashing in the turbulent water struggling to stay afloat. Suddenly, my hand hit solid rock and I was strengthened to hold myself above the waves. There was no land, only this large solid rock in the middle of the ocean. I reached out and grabbed Ann's hand and brought her hand to the rock.

I was puzzled, but I felt very strongly that the Spirit of God had a message for me in this dream. I knew, in God's time, He would show me the meaning. But right now, there were so many hurting people out there and so few laborers to reach them. Ministry consumed my life; I was so busy reaching out to a lost and hurting world that I didn't see what was happening in my own family. There were no evenings left to spend with my wife and children. In addition to working a full time job, Ann cared for our three sons and was left with all the burdens of running a household. She began to battle for my time, but I was pulled in so many directions in ministry that I didn't have the time or energy to do the special things that keep the romance alive in a marriage. We couldn't even sit and talk without what seemed like a hundred other things demanding our attention.

After a while, Ann became frustrated. She felt I had left her behind, and we were no longer partners in ministry. On several occasions I received "emergency" phone calls from members of our Friday night support group during family birthdays and holidays. I felt I was their pastor and if they were facing a crisis, I needed to be there for them; my wife felt that ministry was more important to me than my family. The more frustrated my wife became with me, the more frustrated I became with her.

Satan took advantage of our growing frustration and used it as an open door to create the "perfect storm" in an attempt to destroy our marriage and ministry. The Bible warns in 1 Peter 5:8, "Be sober, be vigilant; because your adversary the devil, as a roaring lion, walketh about, seeking whom he may devour."

Our home became a war zone. I'd be out late doing ministry and when I'd come home, my wife and I would fight. The more we fought, the less able we were to communicate. One morning my wife awoke early from a dream. She was very emotional as she told me that in her dream she felt God was warning her that I would have an affair with one of the lady volunteers who helped at Wings Of Freedom. I responded, "That's ridiculous! I love God and I would never do anything to hurt Him or destroy my testimony!" I was angry that she would even say that.

She tried to warn me that it was dangerous to counsel women alone and that close friendships with other women could lead to an emotional attachment that could lead to other things. I thought, *She don't even know me or understand me. I'm stronger than that. After all God has done in my life, I would never do anything to disgrace Him or the church.*

One night, after I came home late from ministering at the prison, Ann was angry with me. I said, "Well, if you don't want this ministry, I'll just blow it up!" I didn't really mean that—I only spoke it in anger. I was angry with Ann, and I was also angry with my pastor for telling the staff they could no longer help me with the inmate ministry and Friday night support group. Satan was having a heyday with me; he was relentless in his attacks to destroy my ministry and my marriage.

This time, it looked like Satan might succeed in destroying my marriage. I hated the fighting and got to the point that sometimes I'd leave. I began to feel that I had fallen out of love with my wife and that she had fallen out of love with me. Ann and I looked for a counselor who could help us resolve our marital problems, but never found one we could both identify with. As a last resort, we tried going to a married couple in our church who were licensed counselors, but because they were a part of the inner circle of the church, Ann didn't feel free to share her feelings with them. After a while, I stopped trying and began to consider getting a divorce because we were both miserable.

One day while I was at Wings of Freedom, a lady volunteer noticed that I was not my usual bubbly, happy-go-lucky self.

She stopped in my office to ask if I was okay. It was a weak moment for me, and I began to share my problems with her. We became good friends after that. As we shared our disappointments and heartaches with each other, ungodly feelings began to grow between us. I should have been wise enough to run from the relationship, but I felt so alone. I felt that the two most important people in my life had seemingly turned against me—my wife and my pastor—and it was draining me.

One day the relationship that had developed with the Wings of Freedom volunteer got out of hand, and we stepped over the line. The sin left a great "void" inside of me—an emptiness in my heart where once God's Spirit had dwelt and thrived. Now there was only the anguish that King David described after he sinned against God. His agony is recorded in Psalm 32:3–4: "When I kept silent, my bones grew old through my groaning all the day long. For day and night, your hand was heavy upon me; my vitality was turned into the drought of summer." (NKJV)

In the mornings, I'd take our son to the baby sitter after Ann left for work and then go back home and lie on the floor and cry. I was so disappointed in myself. I thought I was stronger than that. I remembered God's warning in 1 Peter 5:8 that the devil, as a roaring lion, is seeking whom he may devour. Ann's advice was right. I had thought her dream was ridiculous. But I learned that none of us are immune to failure and we must be diligent to guard ourselves from being put in a situation where Satan can take advantage of us.

I began to cry out to God to show me how to get back to the place where I could feel His presence and power in my life. I had disgraced the church and the ministry, but most of all I'd been a disgrace to God. My prayer time was lifeless. I could no longer feel God's presence or hear His voice. God's anointing had also left me. I could see on people's faces that God's anointing was on His Word when I preached. God still performed miracles in the lives of those who would receive His Word, but as soon as the sermon was over, I had no power to live the life I was preaching.

One morning, as I lay prostrate on the floor weeping, for the first time in months I heard the voice of God. He gave me two scriptures: Psalms 119:9, "Wherewithal shall a young man cleanse his way? By taking heed therefore to thy Word." and John 17:17, "Sanctify them through thy truth: thy word is truth." I said, "Okay, God, how do I do this? How can I overcome what I've done?" God told me I had to "get back to truth." To get back to truth, I had to repent to those in authority over me. Then, I would have to do what they told me to do. The timeline God gave me to repent to my pastor was after the Angel Tree party on December 16. It was important not to do anything to hurt the success of our church's Christmas outreach of giving gifts to children whose parents were in prison.

The first one I had to repent to was Dave King, Director of Freedom Ranch, Inc. and Wings of Freedom. Then, the day after Christmas, I was to repent to my wife. On December 7, 2001, I met with Dave King and told him the whole story.

Dave was hurt by what I had done, but he told me he loved me and would do everything he could to restore me.

The Angel Tree party was a great success with two local TV stations filming us. The stage was filled with bicycles and other nice Christmas gifts for children whose parents were in prison. We brought in barbeque for four to five hundred people. I was blessed by the kids and the generosity of those who had donated gifts and money, but I was miserable on the inside. I dreaded the meeting with my pastor the next day.

I met with the pastor on Monday afternoon and told him everything. The pastor was quiet for a few moments as he looked down at the floor. Obviously, my confession had taken him by surprise. He told me he would have a meeting with the board and get back to me. On Thursday morning, the pastor called me with the board's decision: I must relinquish my position in ministry and leave the church immediately. I was not allowed to come to the church to clean out my office – the church staff would pack my things and I could pick them up after New Year's Day.

I asked if it would be possible to keep all this quiet until the day after Christmas because that was the day I would tell my wife. The pastor agreed to help me protect Christmas for my family. But, he warned, the congregation would be told what I had done on the Sunday after Christmas.

I hadn't expected such a harsh judgment. My family and I had been in that church for seven years. My children had grown up there. I had worked hard to help build up the congregation, from forty the first time I attended, to over three hundred people consistently on Sundays. I was deeply disappointed and hurt by the board's decision. I knew I would have to step down from ministry for a time, but I had hoped the church would forgive me and help me to be restored. My eyes filled with tears. *Sin comes with a high price tag*, I thought. *I've lost my dignity and disgraced the very things I loved the most—ministry and my family.*

The day after Christmas, I confessed to my wife; she was not surprised by my confession. Even though I hadn't told her what had happened, she knew her dream had been a warning from God. Tormenting thoughts had played havoc with her emotions during the past months. *Dixie is the anointed one*, she thought. *God will answer his prayers, not mine.* She had struggled to strengthen her own relationship with God and learned to depend on her own prayers instead of my prayers. She had prayed God would help her sort through her tormenting thoughts and that the truth would be revealed.

After I confessed to Ann, I told her I would do whatever she wanted me to do, but I felt the best thing would be for me to leave. I told her I didn't think she could ever trust me again and I didn't want us both to be miserable for the rest of our lives. Ann stood her ground. She told me she didn't feel that marriage should be easily thrown away, and that a good marriage is worth fighting for. Ann's mother had been divorced five times, and Ann didn't want our children to experience the anguish of divorced parents.

Even though I didn't feel Ann could ever forgive me, I kept my promise that I would do what she asked me to do regarding our marriage. God showed me there are two parts to forgiveness—there is verbal repentance, and there is a walk of repentance. Both are equally important. Ann and I began marital counseling at Grace Fellowship Church. The first thing the counselor told us was to get the "D" word (divorce) out of our vocabulary. With that settled, we began to work on rebuilding our relationship and learning God's principles for marriage.

The counselor advised us to read a book, *Men Are Like Waffles—Women Are Like Spaghetti*. Through this scripturally based book, we began to understand the differences in the way women and men think and process information, which helped us develop better communication and listening skills. Our homework was to sit on the couch and talk for thirty minutes every day when we came home from work. Praying together was also a must. We were to pray aloud for each other. The prayers really blessed me; I loved hearing my wife pray for me and ask God to bless our marriage.

By God's grace, Ann was able to forgive me. However, it took several months for us to work out our differences and to rebuild Ann's trust in me. Ann and I switched cell phones so she would know that I had nothing to hide about who I talked to on the phone. I also gave her permission to call me at any time and ask where I was and who I was with. My willingness to be transparent helped rebuild her trust.

During the months following my confession to Ann, God gave her grace to walk in agape love (the type of love God gives without expecting anything in return). The Wings of Freedom volunteer struggled emotionally from the aftermath of what we had done and slipped back into using drugs. Ann took in her children and cared for them during the time the volunteer was admitted to a drug facility to get the help she needed.

In her testimony to others, Ann tells how God showed her that she was fighting a spiritual battle based on Ephesians 6:12, "For we wrestle not against flesh and blood, but against principalities, against powers, against the rulers of the darkness of this world, against spiritual wickedness in high places." When Ann counsels with other women, she asks them, "What is your part in the problems between you and your husband?" Ann tells them if they are making their husband's life miserable and if they are not doing the things God says in His Word that a wife should be doing for her husband, then they are a part of the problem. Ann is quick to emphasize that a marriage should not be easily thrown away; a good marriage is worth fighting for.

At the writing of this book, Ann and I are in our twenty-sixth year of a happy, strong marriage. We work together in ministry and our sons and daughters-in-law are involved in ministry with us.

A couple of weeks after my confession became public, the lady administrator of Wings of Freedom asked for a meeting with Dave King, the founder of Freedom Ranch, Inc. Dave had provided the building for me to house the women and children in the program. Dave insisted I go to the meeting with him. The administrator was seated in the office with three other women. She got right to the point, stating that I had caused a black spot on the ministry and asking Dave King to dismiss me and allow her and the women to oversee Wings of Freedom.

Dave let the women have their say, then he spoke up, "Is everyone done now? This is Dixie's vision and I will not remove him. He is going to stay and fulfill his calling. I'm going to support him, and I encourage all of you to get behind him and help him to be healed, restored, and made whole." The administrator resigned and walked out with the other women. Dave turned to me and said, "Okay, now you are the administrator, and I will pay you the salary I paid her." I had lost my salary at the church when I was asked to resign. I thanked God that he had restored the income I needed to provide for my family.

I was humbled by Dave's friendship, his forgiveness, and his willingness to help restore me. I had wanted to give up Wings of Freedom, but Dave and a lady volunteer, Judy, would not let me. Judy insisted, "I'm not quitting and neither are you!" If I didn't show up, my phone would ring. It would be Judy saying, "Dixie, where are you?" I'd say, "Judy, I'm done." She would say, "No, you're not! Now get down here!" She was relentless.

Judy was a blessing from God, but due to health issues, she could not climb the stairs to see what was going on in the apartments. I did not go into the areas of the building that housed the women's living quarters and havoc had broken out on the third and fourth floors. God led me to Barbara, a born-again Christian who was a former inmate and ex-drug addict.

I first met Barbara when I was on staff at the church and she was an inmate at a local pre-release center. One of the women in the center had come to our Friday night support group at the church and later invited Barbara to go. Barbara objected, stating that she had heard some women went to church just to meet a man and she wasn't interested. The woman insisted, "Oh, no, this church isn't like that. The preacher on Friday nights has been in prison and he's real laid back. The sweetest couple, Mary and Maurice, picks us up on Friday nights. You'll love them."

Barbara agreed to come the following Friday and then returned again on Sunday. When Barbara gives her testimony, she tells about the three crosses in the church sanctuary, "When I walked into that sanctuary I saw three crosses. God spoke to me, 'There's a cross for your past, one for your present, and one for your future.' From that point on, I never left God." In her testimony, Barbara states, "Nothing is going to change inside until you find Christ."

For her next two and a half years of incarceration, Barbara never missed a Sunday or a Friday night service. Her mother, who hadn't been in church for many years, started attending the services and became a close friend with Mary and Maurice.

When I learned that Barbara was working at a local Wendy's hamburger restaurant for minimum wage, I felt I could raise enough money to pay Barbara the equivalent salary. I offered her a position as program manager of Wings of Freedom. When I asked Barbara to come help me run Wings of Freedom, she laughingly said, "Yes. No one would know better than me about all the games they play." It didn't take Barbara long to get the havoc under control in the women's quarters. Barbara continues to be a blessing to the ministry and is still program manager for Wings of Freedom today.

By mid-year, I started receiving calls from previous members of my Friday night support group at the church. They asked when I was going to start a church and said they were not going back to church till I started one. I told them they needed to find a church to attend because I didn't know if I would ever start one.

After several phone calls, I prayed and asked God to send me a confirmation if it was His will for me to start a church. I wasn't even sure it was His will for me to oversee Wings of Freedom. I needed to hear from God because some of the people from the church had told me, "Your ministry is over! God can never use you again." Some of the prison chaplains wouldn't even allow me to hold chapel services for the inmates. I oversaw a Bible study at Wings of Freedom, but I didn't really teach them—I just let them share with each other. I hadn't even led anyone to the Lord in the past six months.

In September, a girl who had previously lived at Wings of Freedom ran to the door of my office and hollered, "Dixie. Stay right here. Don't go anywhere!" She ran outside and quickly came back with another girl. "Dixie," she said breathlessly, "My friend wants to be saved, and I don't know how to lead her to the Lord." After counseling her, I asked if she wanted to be saved and she said, "Yes." For the first time in months, I felt the powerful presence of God in the room and heard His voice saying to me, "You can do this!" A word from God was all it took for me. God spoke to my heart, "The gifts and callings of God are without repentance." (Romans 11:29) Regardless of what man had said to me, God had spoken and I never wanted to be out of His will again.

It was settled for me. God's plan was for me to start a church. If we found someone that Jesus didn't die for, they wouldn't be welcome in this church. If Jesus counted them worthy of dying for, then we would welcome them with open arms. Inmates, addicts, prostitutes, sinners, throwaways—all would be welcome in God's church. We would love them and teach them the ways of God.

As I drove home, I remembered what the counselor had told me: "You cannot have a ministry unless your wife is in agreement. Without that agreement, a ministry will not succeed." *I won't make that mistake again!* I said to myself. I had not forgotten the problems I had created by not talking to my wife first when I made the decision to leave my secular job to go into full-time ministry.

I couldn't wait to get home to have our daily thirty-minute conversation the counselor had recommended at the end of each work day. My wife was equally excited when I told her about the girl I'd led to the Lord at Wings of Freedom. Her reply was eight beautiful words, "I think it's time to start the church!" "Praise God!" I shouted. Suddenly, it was like a light came on, and I understood the dream I'd had about Ann and me being thrown into the ocean when our boat sank.

CHAPTER 9

It had been over a year since my dream. I felt sure that the dream was a message from God, but I was puzzled about the meaning. However, I had learned long before not to use human reasoning to figure out God, but to wait on Him; He would reveal what I needed to know when it was time.

In my dream, Ann and I were in a small boat, driving at full throttle in a raging storm. A tidal wave billowed in front of us causing our boat to nosedive into the ocean and never resurface. Ann and I were left thrashing in the turbulent water struggling to stay afloat. Suddenly, my hand hit solid rock. There was no land—only this large, solid rock in the middle of the ocean. I reached out and grabbed Ann's hand and put her hand on the rock.

At the time I had this dream, God was dealing with me to resign from my staff position at the church, but I didn't want to let go of the ministry we had built. Although Ann and I were running at full speed, trying to stay above the storm in our own power, the waves became bigger than us and bigger than our small boat. We lost everything we had built in ministry, but we found each other and a strengthened faith in God.

Ann had been saved when I was in prison, but she felt what we were doing was "my" ministry. Through the storm, she learned that God, the solid rock that saved us in the turbulent ocean, was her strength as well as mine. Previously, Ann had depended on my faith and my prayers to provide our needs; but now she knew there was power in her prayers and that God also speaks to her. Now, to Ann, the ministry was no longer "my" ministry—it was "our" ministry.

When I looked back at our ministry on the church staff, I realized that was the little boat. Now God was showing me He would give us a bigger boat and do so much more through us than we had ever dreamed.

It was around October 1, 2002, when Ann and I started meeting weekly with a group of six other people who were interested in helping us start a church. During this time, we chose the name of the church, the days and times we would hold services, the date of the first service, etc. In the beginning we unanimously voted to name the church "God's Light Shining" in honor of Pastor Ricky, who had faithfully mentored me in prison and in my early days of full time ministry. God's Light Shining was previously the name Pastor Ricky had used for the church he started in Edmond, Oklahoma. He had since changed the name of the church and gave us permission to use the name. Later, we changed the name of the church to God's Shining Light, which remains the name of the church today.

Our goal was to find people who weren't going to church. We did not want to take away from other churches—that was not our purpose. Our purpose was to go out in the trenches and bring in the lost and those who had fallen away from God.

Our first service was to be the first Sunday in January 2003, but as the end of 2002 quickly approached, we still did not have a place to meet. I announced that if we did not have a place to meet by January 1, we would meet in the basement of Wings of Freedom, which would seat about thirty people—maybe forty if we squeezed the chairs close together. Our main problem in not being able to find a place to meet was that we didn't have any money. The only equipment we had to start a church was the CD player we used for music in the Bible studies at Wings of Freedom and some praise and worship CDs.

Three weeks before our first scheduled service, a man I met from another prison ministry walked into Wings of Freedom with donations of food and clothing. He saw me and asked what I was doing now. I told him we were getting ready to start a church. He asked, "Where?" I replied, "I don't know yet. But if we can't find a place by the first Sunday in January, we'll meet in the basement here."

He was involved in an outreach in West Tulsa that met on Friday nights in a warehouse that was set up like a church sanctuary, but they did not have church on Sundays. The man contacted the owners of the building, and they agreed we could meet there on Sundays and pay them $200 a month. Now, we had a nice sanctuary complete with seating, a PA system, and even a pulpit. All we had to bring was our projector and screen so the congregation would be able to see the words to the songs for praise and worship.

Now that the location was settled, we got busy inviting people for our first service on January 5, 2003. I made up business cards with the location and times of services and gave a portion of them to the six people who had been meeting with us to start the church. For the next three weeks, in keeping with our motto, we passed out the cards everywhere we found hurting people. Our God-given motto was and still is: "If we can find someone Jesus didn't die for, then they will not be welcome in our church. If Jesus found them worthy enough to die for, we will welcome them, love them, and teach them the ways of God."

The attendance for our first Sunday service of God's Shining Light Church was sixty-five people, but part of the congregation was friends who came in support. The next week, our congregation dwindled to around thirty-five people. We began to pick up prisoners in the pre-release centers and bring them to church. On Friday nights and Saturdays, we would take food to the homeless and invite them to meet us at a designated place on Sunday to go to church. The church began to grow; by the end of the first year our attendance was between seventy-five and one hundred people every Sunday. It was an exciting time with many being saved, healed, and delivered from drugs and alcohol.

God was equally blessing us and changing lives at Wings of Freedom. We were still in the three-story building in downtown Tulsa with eighteen apartments filled with women who had recently been released from prison, or homeless, or in treatment for drug and alcohol abuse. Several of the women had children who lived with them; our goal was to keep the families together during their recovery and transition back into society.

It was during this time that Crystal came to Wings of Freedom to rebuild her life after she was released from prison. Crystal grew up in California, the youngest sibling in a middle-class family. Both parents worked long hours to provide a nice home and future for their family, leaving Crystal in the care of an older sister much of the time. The family enjoyed many luxuries—a built-in swimming pool, nice home, nice clothes, skiing in the summer, and snowmobiling in the winter.

When Crystal was nine years old, she became sick with flu-like symptoms and a fever. The doctor advised Crystal's mother that she should stay home from school for a few days; however, her mother encouraged her to go to school in spite of the doctor's advice. Crystal, loving school, eagerly agreed. That day, her mother left the family, telling no one she was leaving or where she had gone—an extremely traumatic event for a nine-year-old girl.

Crystal's dad worked long hours and her sister, almost thirteen years older than Crystal, was already out of the home. For the first couple of years, the sister came over to make sure Crystal had breakfast and went to school. After those two years, Crystal had virtually no adult supervision before and after school. At the age of thirteen, Crystal began smoking marijuana with her friends. By the time she was fourteen, she was cutting class and went from being a straight "A" student to a "D" student.

Finally, Crystal was kicked out of school for excessive absences. By now, drugs controlled her life. For the next twenty-three years, Crystal struggled with the roller-coaster ups and downs of trying to get past drug addiction in her own strength. Crystal came to Wings of Freedom on a Greyhound bus from Eddie Warrior Correctional Center on Christmas Eve with a genuine desire to be free from her drug addiction.

Crystal has now been clean and sober for eleven years, her relationship with her children is restored, and her marriage is healed. Crystal is now on staff at Wings of Freedom helping others find restoration and freedom from addiction.

Wings of Freedom is different from other sober-living programs that leave God out of the recovery process. Our goal is to create a controlled environment that is conducive for someone to succeed and put their lives back together; we do not control the people, we control the environment. We have watchmen living on site to maintain our clean and sober environment with safety and security. People choose to live there because they genuinely want to get past their addictions. If a client chooses not to obey the rules, they are asked to leave. The rules include a curfew, getting a job and paying rent, attending twelve-step recovery meetings, and attending Sunday and Friday night church services. Our goal is to give our clients a "hand up—not a hand out."

During the first years of Wings of Freedom, we housed only women and children. A few months after we started God's Shining Light Church, a man walked in with a set of keys. He had watched us grow and wanted to help us start a program for men. I explained there wasn't any money in our budget to start a housing project. He handed me the keys to a three-bedroom house and told me that the house could accommodate up to six men. After I had it filled, I could start paying rent of $700 per month.

A few months later, another three-bedroom house was made available to us to house six additional men in the program. Again, we didn't have the finances to enlarge the men's Wings of Freedom program, but God knew that and had already made a way for us. The owner of the house gave us three months to get set up before we had to start paying rent.

Every step of our growth has been the same—when God gives us an opportunity, we've stepped out, and He has provided the way. I'm sometimes amazed when I look back at my training ground in prison and see how the voice of God led me through each step of preparation for the ministry we are doing today. The eighteen-month business college course God instructed me to complete in prison has given me a foundation of sound business principles on which to build.

One of the men who helped us start the church had previously owned a sprinkler system company. He wanted to start a sprinkler company that would help support the church and provide jobs for people in the Wings of Freedom program. He was willing to run the business, but needed Freedom Ranch's help in getting the equipment. Our business, "Pro Sprinkler" is still operating today.

After about a year and a half, the owner of the warehouse asked that we move God's Shining Light church to another location. We found an empty church on the outskirts of Tulsa that had a sanctuary that would seat around one hundred twenty-five adults with two small bathrooms, but no classrooms for children. We purchased a small building and moved it on site to house our children's program.

Satan took advantage of the confusion of having to find another meeting place to stir up discord among the staff. 1 Peter 5:8 states, "Be sober, be vigilant; because your adversary the devil, as a roaring lion, walketh about, seeking whom he may devour." The problem started with little undercurrents of grumbling among the church staff but had grown to anger and bickering between them. God told me I needed to set up a mandatory staff meeting. The night before the meeting I said, "God, You told me to schedule this meeting, but what am I supposed to say?" He told me to bow down and wash the feet of all the staff members. I wasn't expecting to hear that, but I said, "Okay, God."

At the meeting, I announced that everyone would have their say and would have the freedom to state how they felt. "But first," I explained, "God has instructed me to wash your feet." I opened my Bible to John 13 and read how Jesus became an example to the disciples by bowing down and washing their feet. By the time I prayed for each of them as I washed their feet, everyone was in tears and began hugging each other. After the foot washing, no one wanted to voice their complaints; they all realized we were there to serve. We left the meeting in one accord, focusing on the purpose of our calling.

Although we were averaging between seventy-five and a hundred consistently in our services, we felt we would be able to use the building for at least a year before we would have to find a larger building. However, by the end of our six-month lease, we were bursting at the seams and were forced to look for a larger location.

I found a 5,000 square foot church building at 11th and Hudson in Tulsa with a sanctuary, space for children's church, and an office we could use for Wings of Freedom. The church was on a large lot so we were able to move our company, Pro Sprinkler, onto the church grounds.

We printed business cards with the church's address and times of services and instructed the congregation to give them to everyone they met who was hurting and needed God. The cards were passed out at work, on the street, in liquor stores, and even a drug dealer took some cards. The drug dealer was a relative of someone who attended our church. When the dealer met someone who was struggling to get off drugs, he would hand them a card and say, "Here, if you don't want to do drugs, go to this church." The cards were seeds we planted and God brought in a harvest of lost souls.

The church was going well at this time, but our Wings of Freedom program was facing challenges. Freedom Ranch, Inc., the 501(c)(3) that is the parent company of Wings of Freedom, continued to be plagued with financial problems. Consequently, the apartment building that housed Wings of Freedom was sold by the bank in June, 2003. Wings of Freedom was granted one year before we were required to move out of the building so that the program would not be interrupted. During that year, Dave King, CEO and founder of Freedom Ranch, Inc., received some devastating news. Dave was diagnosed with esophageal cancer. I was heart-broken. I had met Dave when I was in prison and he had continued to be a spiritual father to me after my release and through my early years of ministry. I will never forget the day that Dave handed me a ball of keys and said, "Here, start your housing program." That was the beginning of Wings of Freedom. As his health continued to decline, Dave passed the mantle of Freedom Ranch to me, stating, "Carry on, Dixie, and be the soldier God called you to be." Dave passed away in November of 2004 and I became the CEO of operations and vice president of Freedom Ranch, Inc.

As June 2004 approached, I began looking for an apartment complex to buy to house the Wings of Freedom ladies and their children. I found two apartment complexes about one mile apart that needed work to make them livable. We could use one for the women and their children and the other to house the men in the program. I met with the apartment owner's son and told him about our faith-based program and that we would use the apartments to help people rebuild their lives. But the apartments were under contract with a real estate agent, and with no money for a down payment or closing costs, we were not able to buy them.

One day, in frustration, I asked our program manager, Barbara, if she wanted to keep the program going. Her answer was an immediate "Yes!" I never again considered closing the program to be an option.

In May, we began to move the eighteen women and their children into six houses. Before long, I could see that with the houses spread so far apart, it would be hard for Barbara and me to keep track of everyone. Some of the women weren't abiding by the rules.

About a year after we had looked at the apartments, I received a phone call from the owner. The man was coming to Tulsa and asked me to meet with him. He agreed to a lease-purchase agreement where we would provide the labor, and he would supply the material to remodel the apartments. The apartment buildings allowed us to move all the clients back under one roof; one complex for the men and one for the women.

Having individual apartments with bedrooms and kitchens also allowed us to bring in married couples and married couples with children.

On 11th Street, God's Shining Light Church quickly grew from 125 to 175 consistently and kept growing until there was standing room only on Sunday mornings. Still, they kept coming. They stood along the walls inside the sanctuary and filled the hallway to hear the Word of God. There was an intense hunger for God, and He moved mightily in our services. The altars were filled with people getting saved, healed, and delivered from drugs, hopelessness, anger, hate, alcohol, bitterness, oppression, and depression.

I began to pray, "God, we need more space." As I drove down 11th Street every day on my way to the church, I noticed a partially completed church building. There was never anyone there—just this new building sitting empty. One day I prayed, "God, if it's Your will for us to have this building, You will have to make it happen because we don't have any money." We were out ministering in the trenches and the average annual household income of our congregation was $20,000.

Within thirty days of my prayer, a man came to God's Shining Light Church on a Sunday morning to visit his brother, whom we had brought in from the local pre-release center. The man was amazed with what we were accomplishing and how God moved so mightily in our services. He called me later that same day and asked me to have lunch with him the next week.

At lunch, he asked me two questions: "What are your wants and what are your needs?" I told him we desperately needed more space for the people. He had seen that people were standing inside the sanctuary and outside in the hall to hear the Word of God. I told him I knew of two different buildings that might work for us. He told me he was leaving town to go on a mission trip to Russia and that he would get in touch with me when he returned. He was an eminent businessman in Tulsa and had been very successful in building high-dollar houses.

When he returned from his trip, the businessman brought his wife and children to church on a Sunday morning. After the praise and worship service, I asked if anyone had a short testimony of where they came from and what God had done in their lives.

Davy, a member of the congregation, stood up and shared how God had not only changed his life, but also his wife's life. Davy was a talented musician but had gotten hooked on drugs at a young age. He met his wife Terrie in a bar where he played in the band. Terrie insisted that Davy give up hard drugs before she married him, but in time he pulled her into the world of drugs with him. At the age of forty-seven, Davy was sent to prison for selling drugs.

When I met Davy, he was in the Avalon Correctional Services Center in Tulsa and had come in with the other inmates to our church service. Terrie began bringing their children to the services so they would be able to spend a couple more hours a week with Davy.

Terrie stated that the first three times she walked into the church she was still using drugs. She said her turning point came when I preached on hope on a Sunday morning. She realized that hope was the reason these people had smiles on their faces, not only at the church, but in Celebrate Recovery, which she had started attending with Davy. Terrie realized that she hadn't had hope since she started doing speed twenty-three years prior.

Now, Terrie has a smile on her face. Since she has given her life to the Lord, twenty-two members of her and Davy's family have followed her and Davy in giving their hearts to the Lord and changing their lives. Terrie's smile is the brightest when she tells that ALL of their grandchildren are growing up in the church. Davy now plays bass guitar in Broken Yokes, the praise and worship band at God's Shining Light Church, and manages one of the companies owned by the ministry.

Several other people stood up and told how God had changed their hearts and restored their lives. One lady stood, pointed out the window towards the street, and said, "I used to sell my body out there on 11th Street. Now, I go to church on 11th Street. I just love Jesus, and He has set me free!" God's love had touched her heart and helped her put her old life behind her.

I was troubled to see that the businessman's wife had been crying during much of the service. I hoped we hadn't offended her in any way. I wanted to talk to her after the service but wasn't able to get away from the altar because of so many asking for prayer.

The next morning, I received a call from the businessman. He said he was going down to look at the new church building that was sitting empty on 11th Street and asked me if I wanted to go. When I arrived, the businessman, a real estate agent, and a banker were already there. This was the first time I had seen the inside of the building. The manufacturer's stickers were still on the glass in the windows and the studs were in place, but there was no drywall, plumbing, electrical wiring, heating, or ceilings. Looking up, I could see the rafters and the underside of the roof. *Looks sort of like a replica of Noah's ark*, I thought. I stepped onto the stage and walked to the place where I imagined the pulpit would stand. To me, the building looked huge.

The businessman looked at me and said, "Do you think this would work?" I nodded, "Yes." He turned to the banker and said, "Let's make it happen!"

CHAPTER 10

G od's Shining Light Church was a little over four years old
when we moved into our new building. It had been a busy
eight months since the businessman had signed with us to enter
a lease-option-to-purchase agreement. The agreement stated
that our congregation would provide the labor to finish out the
building, and when we could afford the payments we would
move into the church and purchase it at a fair market value.

Even though we had not yet finished all the classrooms, we
held our first service in the new church on Easter Sunday 2007.
When I drove into the parking lot that morning, the first thing
I saw was a young man about twenty years old. His head was
shaved on each side with a bright orange Mohawk haircut. Even
more shocking than the color, was the twelve-inch tall spikes of
hair down the middle. I shot up a quick prayer to God—well,
really it was more of a question than a prayer—"God, what
have you done?"

When I walked into the sanctuary, there were four hundred
people crammed into a facility built to seat three hundred.
Standing in the pulpit, I looked out at the crowd and thought,
"God, this church isn't big enough!" After the Easter-sized

crowd dwindled to normal, we found we were comfortable in our three-hundred-seat sanctuary.

Mike, the businessman and real estate agent who had helped Wings of Freedom start the second men's house, came to the Easter service with his wife. As we were leaving, I shook hands with Mike and asked him to find out who owned the apartment complex adjacent to the church. The apartments were boarded up and condemned, but with some work we could use them for our Wings of Freedom program. About three weeks later, Mike called and told me he made an offer on the apartments. His plan was to borrow the money to finance the apartments and hire us to do the remodeling work. When the apartments were completed, we would buy the complex and move the Wings of Freedom program into it. He said all that before I could say anything. Without a dime, we put a new roof on the building, remodeled each of the apartments, and began moving in people with broken lives, minds, and spirits.

Now, we had three apartment complexes and a nice church building. Along the way, we had added more businesses to help support the ministry and provide jobs and training for our clients. Life was good, and the ministry was thriving. In our April church board meeting I made an announcement, "I want to get the construction completed on the inside of the church and then, I just want to concentrate on preaching the gospel and reaching the lost—and I don't want any more construction projects." The board unanimously agreed. We thought it was time to settle in and manage what we had going, but God had different plans.

In October 2008, two to three months after we completed the last of the classrooms in the church, the real estate agent who helped us buy the church called me and asked, "Are you still running your housing program?" I told him "Yes." Excitedly, he said, "Well, I have a deal for you…" I interrupted, "I really don't want any deals right now." The agent replied, "Oh, but you need to see this apartment complex." "I really don't want any more apartments," I said. "But," he insisted, "You really want to look at this deal." Every muscle and fiber of my tired body was screaming, "No! You don't want to do this," but I heard the voice of God say, "Ask him for the address." As I drove out of the church parking lot, I thought, *I really don't want to do this!*

As I drove up to the complex, I saw fourteen buildings with new roofs, new windows, and new doors. I could feel the hair standing up on my arms and the back of my neck as if I had been hit with a bolt of static electricity. This apartment complex would allow us to reach more families, keeping them together during the recovery process. The buildings housed a total of fifty-four apartments; sixteen of the apartments were two bedrooms and one was three bedrooms. The interior of the buildings had been gutted, but only eight apartments had been remodeled and finished. The price tag was $550,000, which was less than $8,000 per unit. I prayed, "God, if this is you, you're going to have to convince my wife and my board of directors."

My wife, by then, had a master's degree in accounting. She had already told me, "We're done. We can't do anymore!"

I felt led by God to go pick up my wife and show the apartments to her. As we drove up to the apartment complex, I could see that she was feeling what I felt. Ann looked at me and said, "We can do this." I stared at her in disbelief; I had expected her to say, "No!" and that would put the whole idea to rest. I thought, *God, are You telling me that buying these apartments is Your will?* I had learned to wait for a confirmation from God before stepping out.

One by one, I took each member of the board of directors to see the complex. Each answer was the same: "We can do this." I still get chills when I look back at how my wife and each board member said exactly the same words. A peace settled over me, and I knew God was in it. God knew I would need a strong confirmation from Him to overcome Satan's opposition in the coming months.

I called Mike again, the businessman who had helped me with the apartments adjacent to the church. When he saw the fourteen apartment buildings, he replied, "This is a no-brainer. We can get it done." This was during the time when the economy went bust in 2008, and there were bank failures across the United States; many banks stopped loaning money. We needed to borrow $1,000,000: $550,000 to purchase the complex and $450,000 to renovate the forty-six unfinished apartments. Even though we had three guarantors willing to sign the note, with each of the guarantors worth over a million dollars, we were turned down by five different banks. I went back to God and said, "God, if this is truly Your will for us to buy these apartments for Wings of Freedom, You are going to have to make it happen."

Shortly after that, the bank that owned the property made us an offer: They would loan us the $550,000 to purchase the property, but they would not loan us the money to renovate the unfinished apartments. We would have to come up with that on our own. This wasn't completely the answer I had wanted, but I had total peace in proceeding with the purchase. God had confirmed to me it was His will and I knew He would provide the funds to finish out the apartments even though I couldn't see how.

We signed the loan to purchase the apartments December 31, 2008, and started the renovation project with what little money we had in January, 2009. In February, a couple agreed to allow us to borrow against their $100,000 CD to buy building materials. As we'd finish an apartment, we would fill it. Over the next year, we never ran out of building materials; God was always faithful to provide what we needed. We completely renovated and filled the forty-six apartments by the end of the year.

At the writing of this book, Wings of Freedom now has 107 apartments, and we average between 160 and 170 clients plus their children year-round. Our clients are referred to us from prisons, the county jails, drug and family courts, Department of

Human Services, and other programs. To my knowledge, Wings of Freedom is the only sober living program in Oklahoma—or possibly even in the nation—that provides a facility for families to stay together during recovery.

The rules of Wings of Freedom are set up to help our clients transition back into society by teaching them a "normal" way of life. They are required to stay clean and sober. They get up and go to work and learn to be self-supporting—not relying on a government agency to house and feed them. They go to church, go out to dinner and a movie occasionally, spend time with their children, and go to sporting events or other types of wholesome entertainment. If they have a driver's license and a car, we require them to have auto insurance. If their driver's license is suspended, we encourage them to pay their fines and reinstate their license. We teach them what is acceptable in society to be "normal" and to obey the laws of the land.

Chris is one of our clients who learned the meaning of "normal." Chris was strung out on meth and had set himself on fire after his sons were taken from him by their mother. He barely escaped death and spent an extended amount of time in ICU. He was really messed up from the meth, and he was diagnosed bipolar schizophrenic dual personality. After Chris was dismissed from the hospital, a minister friend introduced me to him and asked me to help him. Chris had already started using drugs again but was crying out for help. I told my friend there was nothing I could do; we were not equipped to handle a mental disability. My friend begged, "Dixie, you are the only one who can help him. Will you just try?" I conceded, "Okay, we'll give it a try if Chris will agree to voluntarily leave if he starts using drugs again." Chris left after three days, but in those three days we planted a seed of hope in his heart that he could have a better life.

About thirty days later, Chris returned and begged me to let him come back, swearing he would not let me down this time. It was exciting to watch Chris' progress as he overcame his drug addiction and grew in his relationship with God. I frequently remind our clients that God loves them and recite John 3:17 to them. "For God did not send the son into the world in order to judge (to reject, to condemn, to pass sentence on) the world; but that the world might find salvation and be made safe and sound through Him." (Amplified version) Chris took this verse literally and set goals for himself to go to school, get his heating and air conditioning license, and come off disability. He not only got his heating and air license, he got a contractor's license and started his own company. Today his sons live with him, and he has married and has a daughter.

Setting the Captives Free revivals are still an important part of the outreach of God's Shining Light Church. These tent revivals are not the ordinary revival services that most churches experience. These services are led by me and four to five former inmates with powerful testimonies of how God changed their hearts while in prison, and how God has restored their lives and given them back their families. George and Corky, who first ministered to me at Conner prison, are part of the group who leads the revivals. As inmates, society considered us hopeless, but God considered us valuable and worthy of sending His only son to die for us.

I was asked by Tony Mac, a former inmate who also gave his heart to God while he was incarcerated, to partner with his ministry, Free in Christ, to hold a revival at Oklahoma State Reformatory in Granite, Oklahoma. Granite is Oklahoma's oldest prison, labeled as a "hotspot," and riddled with angry gang members, frequent fights, and drugs.

Granite has a population of eight hundred men, many serving life sentences without parole for heinous crimes. We set up the tent in a fenced area of the yard—the first revival tent ever to be set up inside the walls of Granite prison. There's always an excitement in the yard when we set up the tent and an anticipation that God is about to do something.

The first night we had 270 men in attendance; the second night, 300; and the third night we had 340 men. Talk about an outstanding praise and worship service—imagine worship led by an Indian band with tom-toms and tribal dancing. The tangible presence of God in the services was indescribable. Rival gang members stood shoulder to shoulder with their arms raised and tears streaming down their faces as they sang over and over, "Jesus Loves Me."

Tears filled my eyes as I looked into their faces. Many, like myself, would not have been there if they had been taught morals or guided in the right direction as a youth. Many of them had grown up in an abusive family in gang-infested neighborhoods with drugs and crime an everyday occurrence. To survive, they were forced to become like those around them.

I didn't want to leave them. I wanted to stay there for hours and pray for them, but it was not allowed. When the guards took the inmates back to their cells, we were required to leave the grounds. But we left them with hope and we left them with God.

Sunday morning services at God's Shining Light Church are the highlight of my week. In my opinion, our praise and worship leaders are among the best in the nation. Our lead and bass guitar players learned to play in bars, but now they rock for Jesus. Our worship service can be described as "enthusiastic" with cheering and whistling a part of our praise to God.

As I look out over the congregation, I see men and women whose hands were once used for crime now raised in praise to God as they sing, "Let My Life Song Sing to You." Men as well as women wipe away tears. Some had become so hardened they had not been able to cry until they met God. Most of the children attend our children's church services, but a few stay in the sanctuary with their parents or grandparents. I love seeing the children, who once lived in abusive environments, swaying to the music with their little arms waving above them. The children are especially precious to me. Just knowing that the cycle of crime has been broken in their lives makes any sacrifice worthwhile.

As I look across the sanctuary, I'm reminded that there are so many miracles in our congregation. Jeff is one of those miracles—a son gone astray, much like the prodigal son in the Bible (Luke 15:11–32). He was raised by devout Christian parents who took him to church two to three times a week. As a young man, Jeff started experimenting with drugs, opening the door to Satan's attack on his life; it was as if all the demons in hell had attached themselves to him. His entire personality changed—he was cruel, and after his Marine Corps training in the Special Forces, he was also dangerous. Eventually, Jeff ended up in prison with a life sentence for murder.

In Jeff's testimony, he states that in prison as the drugs wore off, the Word of God and the things he had learned in church as a child started coming back to him little by little. He quotes God's promise in Proverbs 22:6, "Train up a child in the way he should go: and when he is old, he will not depart from it." Jeff began to read the Bible again and attend the church services at the prison. But after serving twenty years of his sentence, the hopelessness of prison pulled him down and he began using drugs as an escape.

In 2005, Jeff was a participant in the prison riots in Oklahoma and as a result he was then transferred to Oklahoma State Penitentiary in McAlester, Oklahoma to H block, where the most dangerous inmates are kept. In 2007, Jeff was attacked by two inmates and stabbed thirty-seven times. Seven of the thirty-seven stab wounds should have been fatal. He was stabbed in the stomach, spine, both lungs, and an eight-inch knife was thrust into his heart. Jeff was flown by helicopter to a hospital where he underwent multiple surgeries, including open heart surgery. After the surgeries, the doctors stated he would not live.

Jeff's mother came to the hospital, leading Jeff's blind father behind her. She walked up to the armed guards at the door of Jeff's room and announced, "I've come to see my son." A guard stopped her, declaring "You will not go in there! It is against the law and policy." Jeff states that his little mother forcefully replied, "You are not going to stop me!" and pushed her way past the two armed guards. Jeff's eyes fill with tears as he tells how his parents sat by his side. "My mother sat on one side of my bed, and my dad sat on the other side. They prayed life back into my mutilated body. My body was lying in that hospital bed, but my spirit was somewhere far away in the darkness. I could hear my mother and father declaring, 'You will live and not die. You will live and not die.'"

Jeff is alive today, and God has completely healed him. Jeff states in his testimony that there's no one alive that tough or that lucky to live through such a brutal stabbing. He states, "Almighty God kept me alive for a purpose." Jeff was discharged from prison exactly twenty-five years from the date he entered. He has now successfully completed the Wings of Freedom program and is sharing with others what God has done in his life.

Debbie is another one of our graduates of the Wings of Freedom program and is currently a house mother in one of our apartment complexes. Debbie carried a horrible secret into her adulthood. For three years, starting at the age of seven, she was sexually molested and threatened by a family member. She was afraid to tell anyone.

Married at the age of sixteen, Debbie concealed another horrible secret for the next three years of brutal physical abuse from her husband. Debbie took the beatings until the black and blue marks became so severe she couldn't hide them any longer. She left her husband and later got involved with a man who taught her how to sell drugs. Other relationships through the years with men ended in abusive behavior—a pattern Debbie didn't know how to break. Debbie's mother took her to church regularly in her preschool and early elementary school years, but after her dad had an affair and left the family, her mother stopped going to church. Debbie felt God didn't love her and didn't want her because of the lifestyle she had lived.

One final confrontation with a man changed Debbie's life forever. The beatings from this man had continued to worsen, resulting in a hospital stay when he bashed in her head. On more than one occasion, he had threatened to kill her—even holding a gun to her head. This particular day, Debbie and a lady friend were sitting in Debbie's car in the parking lot of a grocery store. Debbie looked up to see the man, who had been beating her, walking across the parking lot. He said he wanted to talk and got into the back seat. Debbie could tell by his eyes he was crazed with drugs.

As the conversation heated up, he hit Debbie a couple of times in the head. Debbie coaxed him out of the car by telling him she would get out also. She opened the front left door and stepped out; he exited the right rear door. She quickly jumped back inside the car, locked the doors, started the car and drove a few feet, but her car stalled preventing her from leaving the parking lot. The man pulled his knife and started towards the car shouting he would kill her. Her friend in the front seat was screaming, "He's going to kill us! He's going to kill us!" "Not this time," Debbie said, as she reached for the gun in her glove compartment. She stepped out of the car, aimed, and shot the man.

Debbie was taken to Tulsa County jail and charged with first-degree murder. Debbie felt God would never forgive her now because she had broken one of the Ten Commandments: "Thou shalt not kill." Debbie was invited by another inmate to a chapel service at the jail. The lady who was speaking in the chapel said, "I don't know why, but this evening I feel led by God to share a different message than I had planned." She told the story of how King David had put Bathsheba's husband on the front lines during a battle and ordered the troops to withdraw, leaving him to be killed. David had done this so he could have Bathsheba for himself, but God forgave David—even for murder. Debbie realized for the first time that God loved her unconditionally. She went back to her bunk and wept over the life she had lived and begged God for forgiveness.

Debbie states that she was told that if she insisted on a jury trial and lost, she would be facing life in prison. Having no money to hire an attorney, she accepted a plea bargain with a forty-year prison sentence. Seventeen years later, Debbie was released on parole and came to Wings of Freedom. Today, Debbie is serving the Lord and is going to college to get a degree in counseling. She has a love for women in recovery who've suffered domestic abuse. Debbie says she has found her purpose, and that purpose is to love those who feel like they've never been loved.

This is what Wings of Freedom is all about—transformation of spirit, soul, and body. God has not called me to go to other nations. He's called me to win the lost in America and in the prison systems. He's called me to place a seed of love and hope in every person's heart that comes through the doors of Wings of Freedom. Many of our clients, like me, did not have the opportunity of growing up in a Christian home that taught them integrity, morals, and read Bible stories to them. The first time I heard the story of Noah's ark and the promise the rainbow represents was in Conner prison. Some of our Wings of Freedom clients were taught about the goodness of God, but like the prodigal son, chose another road—until one day they hit a brick wall and cried out to God.

It's God's agape love that keeps me from giving up when it gets hard, when the ministry funds are low and the bills are piling up, and when someone we've poured our love and support into ungratefully walks away. Everything in me wanted to give up on Johnnie, a client in our Wings of Freedom program, but God wouldn't let me give up on her. It took her five years to graduate a six month program, but today, Johnnie is helping others overcome childhood sexual and physical abuse.

CHAPTER 11

Johnnie was conceived by alcoholic parents. Her father was stabbed and killed three months before her birth by a fifteen-year-old boy over an old tool box in a dumpster. It was a situation that started with, "My big brother can 'whup' your big brother" and her father lost. After Johnnie was born, her mother disappeared into the world of drugs, leaving Johnnie and her two siblings to fend for themselves.

Johnnie almost died twice in the first couple of months. Finally, an aunt and uncle stepped in and took in all three of the children, but in time, the aunt and uncle were divorced. Johnnie was taken away from blood kin and sent into a life of pure hell. Johnnie states that being adopted is not always a good thing. Her adopted mother was very vengeful, but her family was worse—"way worse" as Johnnie puts it. "I became the 'family property' for the next fourteen years— meaning they could and would do anything they wanted to me. I took my first drink at age three—vodka mixed with orange juice. I remember the moment I lost my innocence, and the child inside me shattered and died. It has taken me forty-one years to put that child back together," Johnnie states.

Johnnie remembers the first time she ran away. She states, "The suitcase was bigger than I was." Johnnie became an alcoholic by the time she was in the fourth grade with shakes, tremors, and needing a morning drink to be normal. Over the course of the next decade, Johnnie was moved from place to place, so she never learned to build relationships. By the time she started the twelfth grade, she had been in eighteen different schools.

Johnnie states she took her last beating from her adopted mother at age fourteen and refused to go back home. It was getting hard to hide all the bruises; by now the courts were involved. Everyone was tired of Johnnie's behavior, but no one asked the important question, "Why would a straight A student be so much trouble?"

Although Johnnie had never been taught about God, she knew He had always been there—even when she denied she needed Him. Many times in her young life, Johnnie had faced death and somehow always escaped. She knew, beyond a shadow of a doubt, there was an evil walking this earth. She states, "I had lived with demons all my life, so I knew there had to be a God—there's always two sides of the coin." At age eighteen, Johnnie was told she was dying from "that stuff you've put through your liver for fifteen years—alcohol."

Johnnie later married and was told by the doctor that because of the damage done to her insides as a child, conception would not be possible—she would never have children. Seven years later, Johnnie gave birth to the first of her four children. It was the last child that helped her start the healing process. Her daughter, age three, came running through the house unclothed after a bath. As Johnnie watched her little girl dancing around, as children often do, she had one of those life-changing moments. Johnnie realized there was nothing that baby could do that would make her deserve to have someone take her innocence away. It would not be her fault.

For the first time, Johnnie knew that what her family had done to her was not her fault; they were really sick people who needed help and forgiveness. Johnnie states, "I had carried guilt with me all my life, feeling I was a bad person. I don't know if that makes sense to some, but people who have lived with incest understand this feeling. It is part of the great lie we perpetrate on ourselves—we reason that it could not possibly be the fault of the people who love us; there has to be something wrong with us!"

The haunting memories from Johnnie's past and her drug habit eventually destroyed her marriage and she was on the road again. Johnnie hit bottom—cooking and selling meth, followed by seven years of incarceration. When placed in drug rehab, Johnnie jumped the fence and ran away. She states, "I was on my way to self-destruct. As I walked down the road, I asked God if He was real, and if He was, what did He want from me? From somewhere a voice said, 'Go back!' I stopped in the middle of the road and said, 'What?' as I looked around to see where the voice came from. But there was no one around. I said, 'Wait a minute. I'm not going back! I'm going to go get high—high enough to never have to feel again!' The voice repeated, 'Go back.' For some reason, I listened for once."

In her testimony, Johnnie states, "Since I've given my life to God, I have a peace I can't explain. To say that I got total peace all at once would be a lie. I got it in tiny pieces—a bite at a time. I've had to learn hard-fought lessons of forgiveness of others, but mostly of myself. God has formed me into a decent person now—a person I like. I hated me for so long. Now, I have compassion for people who hurt. I've learned that the aftermath of mental, physical, and emotional abuse can be erased if you simply lay it down at the cross of Jesus. It's real simple. I didn't say 'easy.' If being sober and straight was easy, no one would choose to be a junkie. 'Simple' and 'easy' are two different words—don't confuse them."

I'm so grateful God wouldn't let me give up on Johnnie. Johnnie is now a mentor and house mom at Wings of Freedom. She is in Celebrate Recovery leadership, teaches a class on recovering from sexual abuse, and is nearing completion of a two-year course to become a Christian counselor. Every Saturday night, Johnnie is at the county jail sharing her testimony and is badged by the Department of Corrections to go back into the prisons to share the good news of the gospel of hope with others like her.

I'm also grateful that God didn't give up on me. At the writing of this book, I have been out of prison for twenty years and have not used drugs since God delivered me from this addiction in the Oklahoma County jail in 1987. I am the founding and senior pastor of God's Shining Light Church in Tulsa, Oklahoma; the CEO and VP of Freedom Ranch, Inc.; and the director of Wings of Freedom. I'm still married to my lovely wife of twenty-nine years, Ann, and I am the father of three sons and one daughter. God has blessed us with two wonderful daughters-in-law and six grandchildren. My two older sons, Cory and his wife Casey, and Little Dixie and his wife Amber, are involved in the ministry of God's Shining Light Church. Little Dixie also manages one of the Freedom Ranch businesses that help support the Wings of Freedom program.

God's Shining Light Church is set up as a separate corporation. The church has continued to grow since we moved into our new building in 2007. By 2010, we started two services on Sundays to accommodate the growth of the congregation. Now even with two services, our 11:00 a.m. service is nearing full capacity and we've moved in additional chairs along the sides of the sanctuary.

Not everyone in our church has been in prison or has been an addict. I thank God for those who've come to help us reach the thousands who were not fortunate enough to be born into a family who taught them Christian values. Some become members of God's Shining Light Church to help in ministry, others have helped by providing finances, others pray fervently for our outreach on the front lines. All are appreciated.

Wings of Freedom is incorporated as a 501(c)(3). Under our parent company, Freedom Ranch, Inc., we have started five companies to provide jobs for our Wings of Freedom clients and teach them a trade. The profits from the companies are put back into the program so we can continue to cycle in new people as beds become available.

Many of our clients come to Wings of Freedom with empty pockets and only the clothes on their backs; others have the $50 they were given when they were released from prison. The first thirty days, we have to provide everything for our clients to help them get on their feet: housing, food, clothing, hygiene products, transportation and help with medical care if needed. Imagine the costs of providing everything that 160-170 people need for thirty days, and this process is repeated every time a new client comes to Wings of Freedom.

Some parents pay up to $100,000 to put their children in drug treatment programs that don't have as high of a success ratio as Wings of Freedom. Their success ratio is lower because many of these facilities put people in a box, and they learn to function inside the box for a few weeks or months. When the addict leaves the facility, they have not learned how to function in society. Consequently, the pressures of life drive them back to drugs or their past lifestyle. They don't want to go back, but it's the only way they know how to survive. It's like the children of Israel. After they were freed from slavery, when times got hard, the first thing they wanted to do was to go back to Egypt because they knew how to survive in that environment.

Recovering from addiction is not just about getting past the initial withdrawal from drugs or alcohol; it's about the longevity of the treatment. When someone is making a lifestyle change, coming out of addiction, or being released from prison, there is a process of transformation they must go through. During that process, their environment needs to be conducive for them to succeed, where the drugs, alcohol, or temptation to return to crime is not right there in their face.

During the transformation, they need time to develop new thoughts and habits to change the direction of their lives. They can't just wake up one day and say, "Hey, I know how to live life." They have to learn to be a good husband or wife and a parent to their children; how to live their life with honesty and integrity; how to go to work and be responsible; and learn wisdom to use their money properly, so they won't remain poor.

Currently, the profits from our five businesses are sufficient to enable us to take care of our client's needs for the first thirty days. After that, because of our limited finances, we have no choice but to require them to get a job, start paying rent for their apartment, and provide their own needs. It breaks my heart that many of them have not yet reached a level, physically or emotionally, in thirty days to be able to go back out into society and be successful. When life becomes too hard for them on the outside, they fall back into addiction and their previous lifestyle. In my heart, I know we must do more to break this vicious cycle that will destroy not only our clients' lives, but also their innocent little children who so often fall prey to repeating their parents' downfalls, because that's all they've ever known.

God has put a vision in my heart, a vision I want to share with you and ask you to prayerfully consider becoming a partner with Wings of Freedom. I feel in my heart that God would have us increase the length of the recovery time for our Wings of Freedom clients. Instead of providing all their needs for the first thirty days, we would provide their needs for the first ninety days. Increasing the length of time that we can allow our clients to begin their transition into society will greatly enhance their chances of being successful. The increased recovery time will allow them to focus on spiritual and emotional healing and deliverance from their past. The most powerful factor in the change God made in my life was that when I was in prison, I had time to read God's Word and allow it to change me from the inside out. God's Word changed everything about me— most importantly my mindset.

After a client's initial recovery period of three to six months, my vision is to give them jobs in the businesses owned by the ministry to train and condition them to go back out into society and to take pride in supporting themselves. In the final phase of the nine to twelve-month program, we would move them to a job on the outside, and they would give back to the new ones coming into the program by mentoring them.

It's still amazing to me how God has continuously blessed God's Shining Light Church and Wings of Freedom with miracle after miracle as we've gone about doing the Father's business. Jesus states the importance of being about the Father's business in Luke 2:49, "Did you not see and know that it is necessary as a duty for Me to be in My Father's house and occupied about my Father's business?" (Amplified version). Jesus' example of what it means to be about the Father's business is stated in Luke 4:18, "...preach the gospel to the poor ... heal the brokenhearted ... preach deliverance to the captives ... recovering of sight to the blind ... and to set at liberty them that are bruised."

You may not be able to go to the prisons, or you may not feel called and equipped to go out in the trenches and preach the gospel. You can still be about the Father's business by partnering with Wings of Freedom with your prayers and a monthly gift of whatever God puts on your heart to give. There are so many more like Johnnie, Jeff, Chris, and others who are crying out to God to show them how to change their lives.

Drugs and crime have affected all of us in one way or another. Many have family members or have friends whose family members have fallen captive to the demonic destruction of addiction or crime. I believe it is God's people who are responsible to stand up and fight against this epidemic of evil. If we don't fight against it, it will continue to get worse. Just as God has blessed God's Shining Light Church and Wings of Freedom, I know God will also bless you and meet your needs as you also go about the "Father's business."

I pray this book has been a blessing to you. I ask you to prayerfully consider becoming a partner with Wings of Freedom to help us "set at liberty them that are bruised." (Luke 4:18) On the final page of this book, I have included a tear-out sheet for you to return to us if you would like to be a partner in this ministry or receive future mail-outs to keep you updated on the move of God currently taking place in the prisons and Wings of Freedom. Also, please share your prayer requests so we can pray for you. I have provided a space on the page for your comments. I would love to hear your story of how God has touched your life or the lives of those you love through this book. MAY GOD BLESS AND KEEP YOU AND YOUR LOVED ONES AS YOU SERVE HIM.

CHAPTER 12

———❦———

IF HE DID IT FOR ME, HE CAN DO IT FOR YOU

Just as God changed my life, He can change yours.

When Preacher Budd stormed into my cell in the Oklahoma County jail and shouted, "I came here to tell you God loves you," my heart was opened and I felt I was receiving a message from God for the first time in my life. Then he read John 3:16, "For God so loved the world, that He gave His only begotten Son, that whosoever believeth in Him should not perish, but have everlasting life." He continued with John 3:17, "For God sent not His Son into the world to condemn the world; but that the world through Him might be saved."

Suddenly, I realized that God was not looking down from heaven condemning me. He sent His Son, Jesus, to be humiliated, beaten, and crucified on a cross so I could be spared from the penalty I deserved. That's love! With tears streaming down my face, I went forward to pray and give my life to Christ. As I prayed, all the darkness left me. I felt such peace and joy—even in a county jail.

Even when we know our deepest need is God, we often try wrong ways of getting to know Him. Some of the wrong things people do and say are:

My mother was a Christian so...

It doesn't matter what I believe, just be sincere...

I'll give up all my bad habits...

I'll work real hard and earn it...

I'll be religious and go to church...

None of the above will give us entrance into heaven. Jesus said in John 14:6, "I am the way, the truth, and the life. No one comes to the Father except through me." (NKJV) Jesus is the only sacrifice that was ever given for our sins. A person can have differing beliefs about doctrine, but a person has to receive Jesus as their sacrifice for sins in order to go to heaven.

I Timothy 2:5 states, "For there is one God and one mediator between God and men, the man Christ Jesus." (NKJV)

Romans 6:23 says, "For the wages of sin is death, but the gift of God is eternal life in Christ Jesus our Lord." (NKJV)

God has already done His part to restore our relationship to Him. He took the initiative. Now He waits for each of us to individually accept what He has done for us.

1. **First, we must admit that God has not been first in our lives and ask Him to forgive our sins. I John 1:9**

states, "If we confess our sins, He is faithful and just to forgive us our sins and to cleanse us from all unrighteousness." (NKJV)

2. **Next, we must believe that Jesus died to pay for our sins and that He rose again from the dead, on the third day, and is alive today.** Romans 10:9 says, "That if you confess with your mouth the Lord Jesus and believe in your heart that God has raised Him from the dead, you will be saved." (NKJV) The Bible also says in Acts 4:12, "Nor is there salvation in any other, for there is no other name under heaven given among men by which we must be saved." (NKJV)

3. **Third, we must accept God's free gift of salvation. Don't try to earn it. Our relationship with God is not restored by anything we do, but on the basis of what Jesus has already done.** Ephesians 2:8–9 says, "For by grace you have been saved through faith, and that not of yourselves; it is the gift of God, not of works, lest anyone should boast." (NKJV)

4. **Finally, invite Jesus Christ to come into your life and be the director (Lord) of your life.** Romans 10:11-13 states, "For the Scripture says, 'Whoever believes on Him will not be put to shame.' For there is no distinction between Jew and Greek, for the same Lord over all is rich to all who call upon Him. For whoever calls on the name of the Lord shall be saved." (NKJV)

If you are ready to pray and give your life to Christ, pray the following prayer from your heart:

Father, I come to You in the name of Jesus. You said in your Word that if I confess my sins, You are faithful and just to forgive me of my sins and to cleanse me from all unrighteousness.

Therefore, I confess I have sinned against You. I have done wrong in Your sight and I ask You by the blood of Jesus to forgive me.

I repent for all my wrongs, and I cry out for Your mercy upon my soul. I plead the blood of Jesus upon my soul to cleanse me and to make me whole.

Father, You said in Your Word that if I confess with my mouth the Lord Jesus and believe in my heart that You raised Him from the dead, I shall be saved.

With my heart, I believe You raised Jesus from the dead and with my mouth I confess Jesus Christ as my Lord and my Savior. Father, come into my heart and make me the person You want me to be.

Thank you, Father, for coming into my life. In Jesus' name. Amen.

If you prayed this prayer and meant it in your heart, you are now a child of God. He now looks at you, not for who you were, but for who you are now—His child. John 1:12-13 gives us this assurance, "But as many as received Him, to them He gave the right to become children of God, to those who believe in His name: who were born, not of blood, nor of the will of the flesh, nor of the will of man, but of God." (NKJV)

After I accepted Jesus as my Savior, Preacher Budd explained to me that what had just happened was like a baby had entered my heart, but it was up to me to make him grow. The only way to make that baby grow was to feed him the Word of God. I began reading God's Word every day—every spare moment I had—and soon the baby inside me started growing. Every time I opened the Scriptures, it wasn't about religion. It was about a relationship with God and knowing my Heavenly Father loved me and that His love for me was greater than anything this world had to offer.

Perhaps you are hesitant to pray the prayer of salvation because you are wondering if there really is a God. I challenge you: For one year, separate yourself from the things of the world and seek after the Lord. Read your Bible, pray, go to church, and ask the Lord to show Himself in your life. What have you got to lose? If at the end of that year, you still feel God has not proved Himself to you, you can always go back to your old lifestyle.

I am confident that God will "show up" for you if you mean it in your heart when you pray. The Bible says, "For the eyes of the Lord run to and fro throughout the whole earth, to show Himself strong on behalf of those whose heart is loyal to Him." (2 Chronicles 16:9) (NKJV) The Bible says in 2 Peter 3:9 that God does not want any of us to perish: "The Lord is not slack concerning His promise, as some men count slackness; but is longsuffering to us-ward, not willing that any should perish, but that all should come to repentance." (NKJV)

My prayer for you is found in Ephesians 1:17-23 (NKJV):

17 That the God of our Lord Jesus Christ, the Father of glory, may give to you the spirit of wisdom and revelation in the knowledge of Him,

18 the eyes of your understanding being enlightened; that you may know what is the hope of His calling, what are the riches of the glory of His inheritance in the saints,

19 and what *is* the exceeding greatness of His power toward us who believe, according to the working of His mighty power

20 which He worked in Christ when He raised Him from the dead and seated *Him* at His right hand in the heavenly places,

21 far above all principality and power and might and dominion, and every name that is named, not only in this age but also in that which is to come.

22 And He put all *things* under His feet, and gave Him *to be* head over all *things* to the church,

23 which is His body, the fullness of Him who fills all in all.

NAME _____

ADDRESS_____

CITY _____ STATE _____

ZIP _____

PRAYER REQUESTS _____

_____

_____

_____ YES! I want to become a partner with Wings of Freedom to help win the lost and help restore broken lives, minds, and spirits. I commit to sending a gift of $_____ each month. Enclosed is my first gift of $_____.

_____ I am enclosing a one-time gift today of $ _____.

_____ My gift of $_____ is being made on the website www.gslchurch.com.

God's Shining Light Church
9897 E. 11th St., Tulsa, Oklahoma 74128
Phone: 918-836-7788
Website for Church: www.gslchurch.com
Website for Wings of Freedom: www.wingsoffreedomok.com

Your prayers and gifts are very much appreciated.

Mailing Address
God's Shining Light Church
P.O. Box 690657
Tulsa Ok 74169